INDEPENDENT STUDY ENRICHMENT PROJECTS

Ready-to-Use Projects for Grades 3-8

Teddy Meister and Ann M. Simpson

Illustrated by Eileen Gerne Ciavarella

THE CENTER FOR APPLIED
RESEARCH IN EDUCATION
West Nyack, New York 10995

Library of Congress Cataloging-in-Publication Data

Meister, Teddy.
  Independent study enrichment projects.

  1. Independent study.   2. Project method in teaching.
I. Simpson, Ann M.   II. Title.
LB1601.3.M45   1988   372.13'943   87-24987
ISBN 0-87628-447-0

ISBN 0-87628-447-0

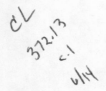

**THE CENTER FOR APPLIED
RESEARCH IN EDUCATION**
BUSINESS & PROFESSIONAL DIVISION
A division of Simon & Schuster
West Nyack, New York 10995

Printed in the United States of America

To Seymour and Charles,
who provided continuous encouragement,
support, and enthusiasm for this project.

About the Authors

Teddy Meister, M.A., University of Central Florida (Orlando), has taught students in both elementary and gifted education for the past 19 years. She has written several books, and articles for such professional magazines as *Instructor* and *Challenge.*

Ann M. Simpson, M.A., University of Central Florida, has been involved with elementary and gifted education for 22 years. She has also been involved in curriculum writing, as well as writing for professional magazines.

Both authors have also conducted many in-service workshops at district, state, and national levels, and served as instructors for college-level courses.

About This Book

"I'm finished. What do I do next?" If you've ever had to scramble about trying to come up with interesting and meaningful activities for students asking this question, you'll welcome *Independent Study Enrichment Projects: Ready-to-Use Projects for Grades 3-8*. This activity book is designed to provide you with creative and unusual exploratory topics related to the following academic areas:

Section 1: FROM CAVES TO SPACE (Science Projects)

Section 2: WONDERS OF THEN AND NOW (Social Studies Projects)

Section 3: NUMBER MAGIC (Math Projects)

Section 4: A WORLD OF WORDS (Language Arts Projects)

Section 5: WORDS IN PRINT (Library Projects)

Each section is multidisciplinary and challenging to students of all ability levels in grades 3-8. All of the projects are easily adapted to any one of these uses:

- independent student research
- small-group involvement
- classwide study units
- learning center activities
- bulletin board displays
- academic exploration
- enrichment homework
- community involvement

The 36 projects can be duplicated for student use to serve as a research guide throughout the topic study. Each project is divided into four parts that are easily identified by symbols:

1. The CONTRACT includes a brief discussion of the topic, followed by places for the student to record selected Target Activities, Spinoffs, and Take Action choices. A contract statement for dates and signatures is included at the bottom.

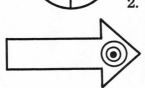

2. The TARGET ACTIVITIES in each project give the student a choice of four research activities related to the topic. The student is to select one or more of these activities and record the choices on the Contract page. Each Target Activity is identified with a circled number and provides easy-to-follow student directions for carrying out a different research activity related to the topic.

3. The SPINOFFS page gives the student a choice of topics for conducting further research as a required or optional activity. You or the student may suggest additional topics. The student's choice should be recorded inside the Spinoffs symbol on the Contract.

4. The TAKE ACTION page provides an optional culminating activity related to the project for use as enrichment homework or community involvement. The student is guided in such activities as taking a field trip, arranging for a class speaker, or conducting an interview or survey. The student's choice should be recorded inside the Take Action symbol on the Contract.

You'll find that all academic areas are enhanced by *Independent Study Enrichment Projects* as students explore the topic of their choice, gather the needed data, and organize their information to communicate it effectively to others.

Teddy Meister
Ann M. Simpson

Contents

About This Book v

Section I   **FROM CAVES TO SPACE (Science Projects)** 1

     I-1 Ballooning • 2

        Contract • Target Activity 1 • Target Activity 2 •
        Target Activity 3 • Target Activity 4 • Spinoff
        Selections • Take Action

     I-2 Caves • 9

        Contract • Target Activity 1 • Target Activity 2 •
        Target Activity 3 • Target Activity 4 • Spinoff
        Selections • Take Action

     I-3 Flight • 16

        Contract • Target Activity 1 • Target Activity 2 •
        Target Activity 3 • Target Activity 4 • Spinoff
        Selections • Take Action

     I-4 Model Rocketry • 23

        Contract • Target Activity 1 • Target Activity 2 •
        Target Activity 3 • Target Activity 4 • Spinoff
        Selections • Take Action

     I-5 Submarines • 30

        Contract • Target Activity 1 • Target Activity 2 •
        Target Activity 3 • Target Activity 4 • Spinoff
        Selections • Take Action

     I-6 Telescopes • 37

        Contract • Target Activity 1 • Target Activity 2 •
        Target Activity 3 • Target Activity 4 • Spinoff
        Selections • Take Action

I-7 Tomorrow • 44

Contract • Target Activity 1 • Target Activity 2 •
Target Activity 3 • Target Activity 4 • Spinoff
Selections • Take Action

Section II   WONDERS OF THEN AND NOW (Social Studies Projects) ... 51

II-1 Borrowed Customs • 52

Contract • Target Activity 1 • Target Activity 2 •
Target Activity 3 • Target Activity 4 • Spinoff
Selections • Take Action

II-2 Castles • 59

Contract • Target Activity 1 • Target Activity 2 •
Target Activity 3 • Target Activity 4 • Spinoff
Selections • Take Action

II-3 Famous Landmarks • 66

Contract • Target Activity 1 • Target Activity 2 •
Target Activity 3 • Target Activity 4 • Spinoff
Selections • Take Action

II-4 Historical Ships • 73

Contract • Target Activity 1 • Target Activity 2 •
Target Activity 3 • Target Activity 4 • Spinoff
Selections • Take Action

II-5 Maps and Map History • 80

Contract • Target Activity 1 • Target Activity 2 •
Target Activity 3 • Target Activity 4 • Spinoff
Selections • Take Action

II-6 Museums • 87

Contract • Target Activity 1 • Target Activity 2 •
Target Activity 3 • Target Activity 4 • Spinoff
Selections • Take Action

II-7 Rivers • 94

Contract • Target Activity 1 • Target Activity 2 •
Target Activity 3 • Target Activity 4 • Spinoff
Selections • Take Action

II-8 Wonders of the Ancient World • 101

Contract • Target Activity 1 • Target Activity 2 •
Target Activity 3 • Target Activity 4 • Spinoff
Selections • Take Action

Section III   NUMBER MAGIC (Math Projects) **109**

III-1 Architecture • 110

Contract • Target Activity 1 • Target Activity 2 •
Target Activity 3 • Target Activity 4 • Spinoff
Selections • Take Action

III-2 Bridges • 117

Contract • Target Activity 1 • Target Activity 2 •
Target Activity 3 • Target Activity 4 • Spinoff
Selections • Take Action

III-3 Camping • 124

Contract • Target Activity 1 • Target Activity 2 •
Target Activity 3 • Target Activity 4 • Spinoff
Selections • Take Action

III-4 Making Games • 131

Contract • Target Activity 1 • Target Activity 2 •
Target Activity 3 • Target Activity 4 • Spinoff
Selections • Take Action

III-5 Math-E-Magic • 138

Contract • Target Activity 1 • Target Activity 2 •
Target Activity 3 • Target Activity 4 • Spinoff
Selections • Take Action

III-6 Optical Illusions • 145

Contract • Target Activity 1 • Target Activity 2 •
Target Activity 3 • Target Activity 4 • Spinoff
Selections • Take Action

III-7 The Stock Market • 152

Contract • Target Activity 1 • Target Activity 2 •
Target Activity 3 • Target Activity 4 • Spinoff
Selections • Take Action

Section IV   **A WORLD OF WORDS (Language Arts Projects)** **159**

IV-1 Advertising • 160

Contract • Target Activity 1 • Target Activity 2 •
Target Activity 3 • Target Activity 4 • Spinoff
Selections • Take Action

IV-2 Mythology • 167

Contract • Target Activity 1 • Target Activity 2 •
Target Activity 3 • Target Activity 4 • Spinoff
Selections • Take Action

IV-3 -Ologies • 174

Contract • Target Activity 1 • Target Activity 2 •
Target Activity 3 • Target Activity 4 • Spinoff
Selections • Take Action

IV-4 -Onics • 181

Contract • Target Activity 1 • Target Activity 2 •
Target Activity 3 • Target Activity 4 • Spinoff
Selections • Take Action

IV-5 Palindromes • 188

Contract • Target Activity 1 • Target Activity 2 •
Target Activity 3 • Target Activity 4 • Spinoff
Selections • Take Action

IV-6 Phobias • 195

Contract • Target Activity 1 • Target Activity 2 •
Target Activity 3 • Target Activity 4 • Spinoff
Selections • Take Action

IV-7 Rainbows • 202

Contract • Target Activity 1 • Target Activity 2 •
Target Activity 3 • Target Activity 4 • Spinoff
Selections • Take Action

Section V **WORDS IN PRINT (Library Projects)** **209**

V-1 Books and Printing Through the Ages • 210

Contract • Target Activity 1 • Target Activity 2 •
Target Activity 3 • Target Activity 4 • Spinoff
Selections • Take Action

V-2 Classics • 217

Contract • Target Activity 1 • Target Activity 2 •
Target Activity 3 • Target Activity 4 • Spinoff
Selections • Take Action

V-3 Fairy Tales, Fables, Folk Tales • 224

Contract • Target Activity 1 • Target Activity 2 •
Target Activity 3 • Target Activity 4 • Spinoff
Selections • Take Action

V-4 Famous Libraries • 231

Contract • Target Activity 1 • Target Activity 2 •
Target Activity 3 • Target Activity 4 • Spinoff
Selections • Take Action

V-5 Magazines • 238

Contract • Target Activity 1 • Target Activity 2 •
Target Activity 3 • Target Activity 4 • Spinoff
Selections • Take Action

V-6 Newbery and Caldecott Award Winners • 245

Contract • Target Activity 1 • Target Activity 2 •
Target Activity 3 • Target Activity 4 • Spinoff
Selections • Take Action

V-7 Poets and Poetry • 252

Contract • Target Activity 1 • Target Activity 2 •
Target Activity 3 • Target Activity 4 • Spinoff
Selections • Take Action

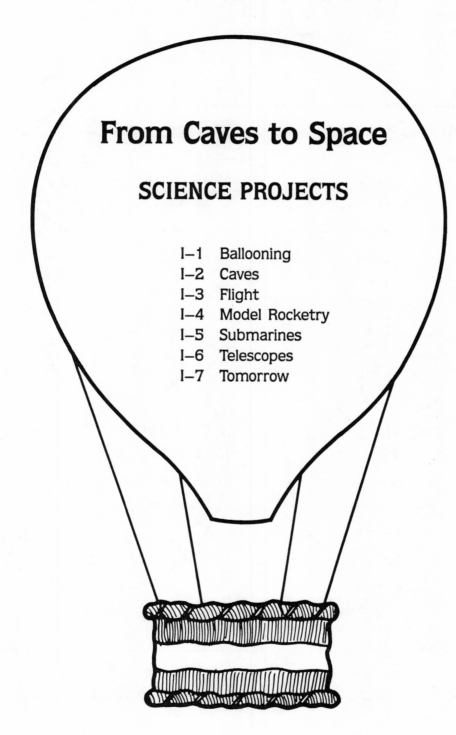

From Caves to Space

SCIENCE PROJECTS

I–1   Ballooning
I–2   Caves
I–3   Flight
I–4   Model Rocketry
I–5   Submarines
I–6   Telescopes
I–7   Tomorrow

CONTRACT

"Up, up, and away" is the thought that comes to mind when we think of the sport of ballooning. Ever since the Middle Ages, people have thought about the use of a "globe" as a machine to lift them high into the atmosphere. Since the late 1700s, when ballooning became a successful experiment in flight, they have been used for scientific research to gather weather data, military defense for spotting enemy positions, and recreation for balloon enthusiasts.

My Target activities will be:

_____

_____

_____

My Spinoffs will be:

_____

_____

_____

I will Take Action by:

_____

_____

_____

My study will begin on _____.

Date

My goal is to finish by _____.

Date

_____   _____
Student Signature   Teacher Signature

TARGET ACTIVITY

Write facts about an important event in the history of ballooning in the design below. Cut several patterns of this balloon for other facts you may find.

1

Year:
Event:
People Involved:
Location:
Purpose:

Arrange your fact balloons in order from the earliest event to the most recent one. Paste them in this order on a large sheet of blue paper. Draw in some background and scenery so it will look like a balloon race. Then display your mural so others can read about your "Balloon History Events."

TARGET ACTIVITY

Use the charts below to compare special features of a manned balloon and a blimp. Consider features such as steering, power source, range, altitude, and designs.

②

Manned Balloon	Blimp

Make cutouts of a blimp and a manned balloon on posterboard. Use these to display your facts listed on the charts above.

TARGET ACTIVITY

List verbs, adjectives, and adverbs that describe the movements of a manned balloon, from lift-off to landing, on the shapes below.

③

Use these words to write a story about a balloon adventure. Make a balloon-shaped booklet of your thoughts for your classmates to read and enjoy.

TARGET ACTIVITY

Create a futuristic balloon in the space below. Design an advertisement that calls attention to its new features and uses.

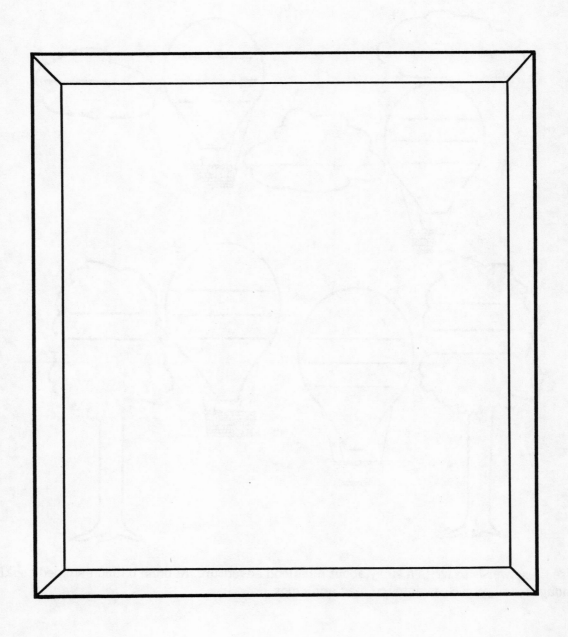

SPINOFF SELECTIONS

Select one of these topics for further research about ballooning.

Blimp	Aviation	Balloon styles
Dirigible	Atmosphere	Hydrogen/Helium
Hindenburg	Balloon Clubs	Jacques and Joseph Montgolfier
Goodyear Blimp	Air Pressure/Air	Jules Verne

Use this space to record your information.

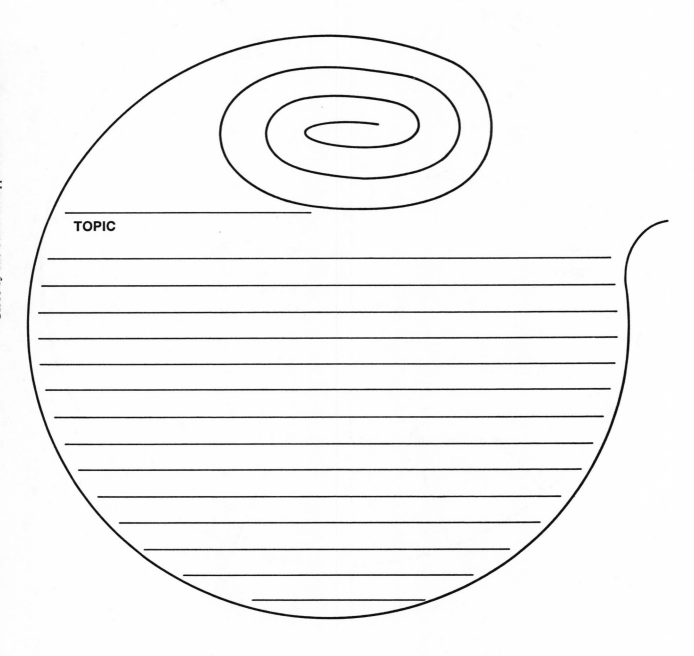

TOPIC

TAKE ACTION

Jules Verne's *Around the World in 80 Days* is a story about a global balloon race at the turn of the century. Find the book in a library and read about this adventuresome flight.

After reading, prepare a dramatization for your class based on some of the events in the story. Use the form below to develop your ideas.

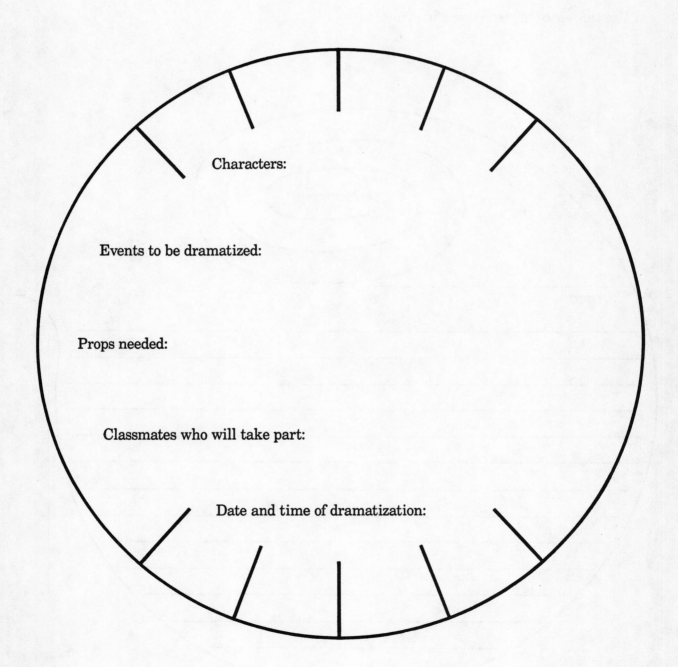

Characters:

Events to be dramatized:

Props needed:

Classmates who will take part:

Date and time of dramatization:

CONTRACT

Nature is constantly at work in the ground underneath our feet. The forces of erosion and shifts in the earth have formed many caves all over the world. People have been fascinated by their dark and twisting mysteries so much that a specialized sport—spelunking—has been developed just for the purposes of cave exploring.

My Target activities will be:

_____

_____

_____

My Spinoffs will be:

_____

_____

_____

I will Take Action by:

_____

_____

_____

My study will begin on _____.

Date

My goal is to finish by _____.

Date

_____   _____
Student Signature   Teacher Signature

TARGET ACTIVITY

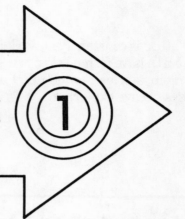

Find out about two famous cave sites in your area or in your country and create a billboard advertisement for each. Locate these cave sites on a map.

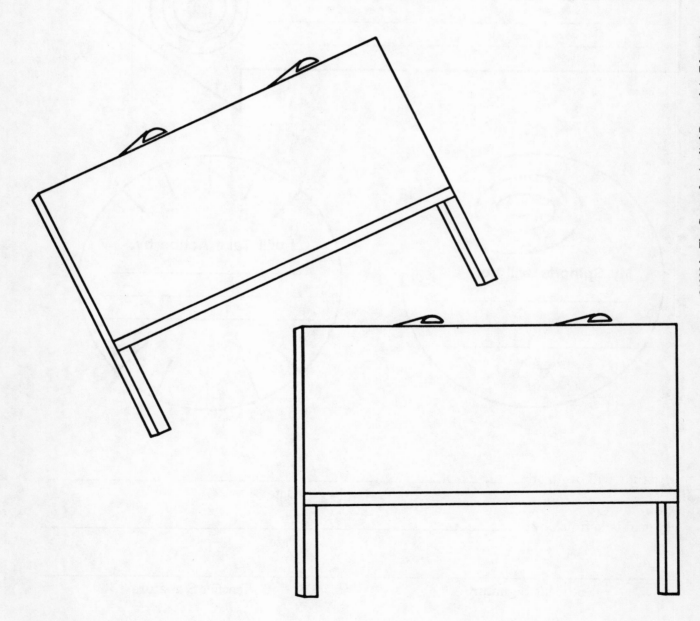

TARGET ACTIVITY

Plants and animals that live in caves must be able to survive in darkness. Draw pictures of some of these unusual life forms and explain the method each uses to adapt to this strange environment.

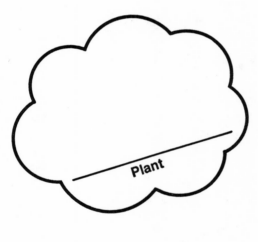

Plant

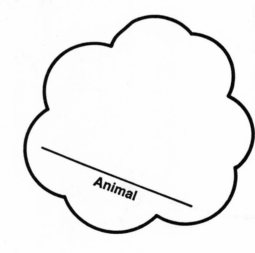

Animal

Animal

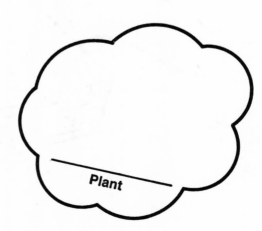

Plant

TARGET ACTIVITY

Pretend you are the "voice" of a famous cave. Tape record your life story and outstanding features. Add sound effects for a more interesting recording!

"I am a cave!"

TARGET ACTIVITY

Construct a three-dimensional model showing the nature-created forms that develop in caves. Share this model and the tape from Target Activity 3 at a learning center.

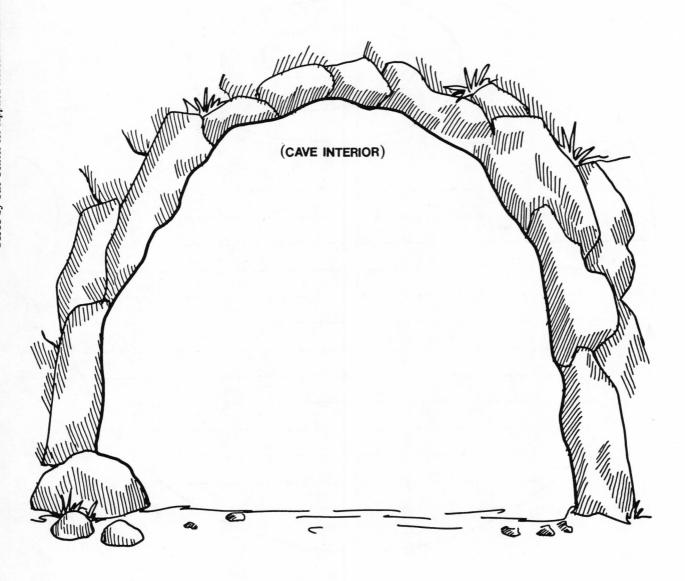

(CAVE INTERIOR)

SPINOFF SELECTIONS

Select one of these topics for further research about caves.

Mammoth Cave	stalagmite	limestone
Carlsbad Caverns	stalactite	Sea Lion Caves, Oregon
Lascaux Cave, France	pictograph	archaeology
Mesa Verde National Park	echo	Mount Rainier National Park Ice Caves

Use this space to record your information.

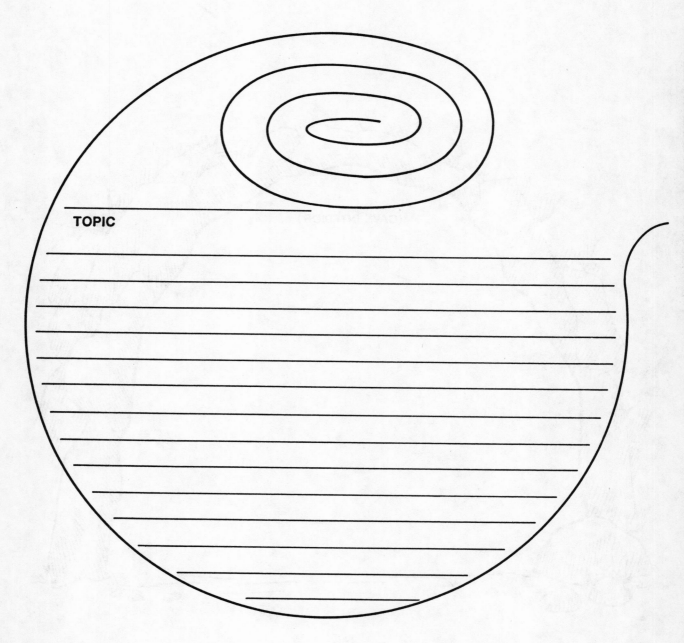

TOPIC

TAKE ACTION

If you would like to know more about the sport of spelunking, write a letter to the following address:

National Speleological Society
Cave Avenue
Huntsville, AL 35810

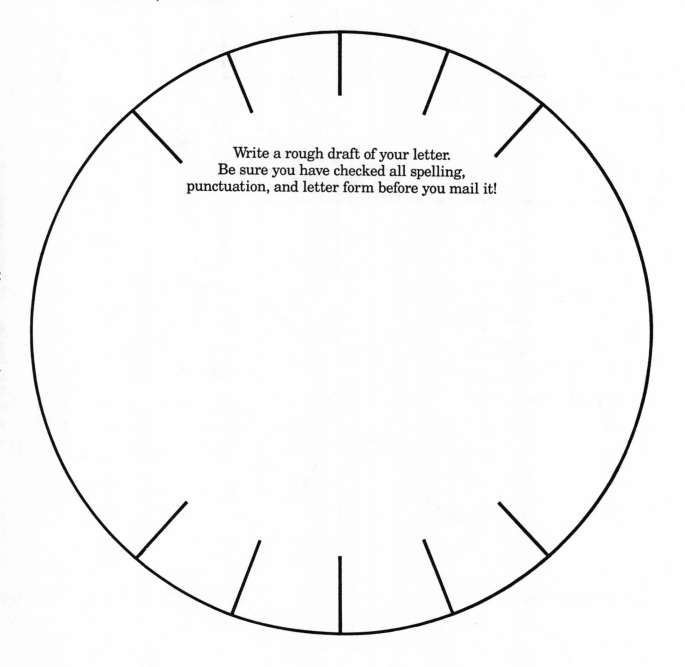

Write a rough draft of your letter.
Be sure you have checked all spelling,
punctuation, and letter form before you mail it!

Do you have any cave sites in your area? If you do, write for additional information!

CONTRACT

To soar like an eagle, and touch the clouds; to see earth from above as you ride the wind!

People observed the birds and dreamed about flying during the early centuries. Many first attempts were disastrous and comical, yet sparked the continuing curiosity of others who made lasting contributions to aviation as we know it today. Air flight has shortened the globe and given us a chance to fly with the birds.

My Target activities will be:

_____

_____

_____

My Spinoffs will be:

_____

_____

_____

I will Take Action by:

_____

_____

_____

My study will begin on _____.

Date

My goal is to finish by _____.

Date

_____   _____

Student Signature   Teacher Signature

TARGET ACTIVITY

Construct a time line showing major events contributing to the development of flight.

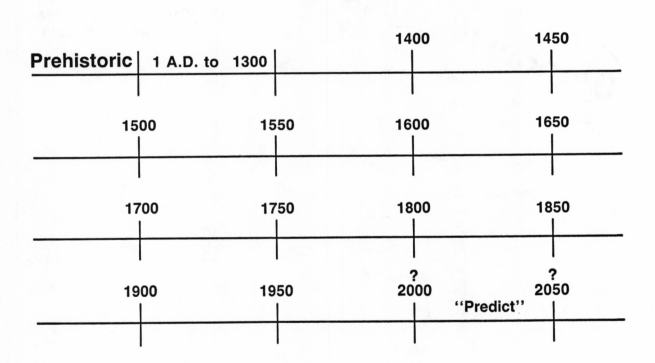

Add other historical events to your time line.

TARGET ACTIVITY

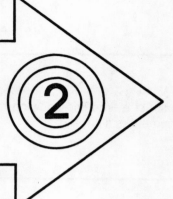

Jakob Bernoulli was a famous mathematician and scientist who developed many principles of flight. Do some research about his life and describe his ideas.

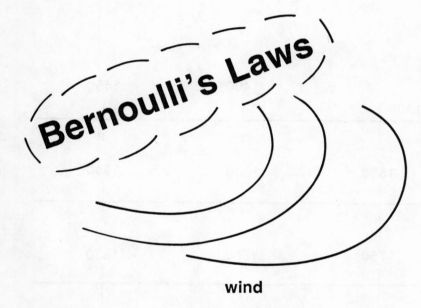

Bernoulli's Laws

wind

currents

lift

drag

**The Life and Times
of Jakob Bernoulli**

Draw diagrams to show some of Bernoulli's principles.

TARGET ACTIVITY

A time capsule about aviation is being readied for opening in the year 2100! You have been asked to collect 10 items for the capsule. List the items and a reason for collecting each one.

Items	Reasons

TARGET ACTIVITY

What personality traits are necessary for a pilot? List the traits. Rank them on a scale of 1 to 10 with 1 being the most important, 2 the next important, and so on. Explain why you think your choices for 1, 2, and 3 are the most necessary.

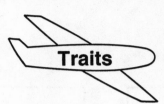

Traits

★ 1. _____
★ 2. _____
★ 3. _____
  4. _____
  5. _____
  6. _____
  7. _____
  8. _____
  9. _____
10. _____

These traits are necessary because _____

_____

_____

_____

_____

SPINOFF SELECTIONS

Select one of these topics for further research about flight.

Pegasus, Icarus, Daedalus   Wright Brothers   test pilots
archeopteryx   Amelia Earhardt   The Spruce Goose
aeronautics   Charles Lindbergh   Concorde
jet power   Leonardo daVinci   Air Force "Thunderbirds"

Use this space to record your information.

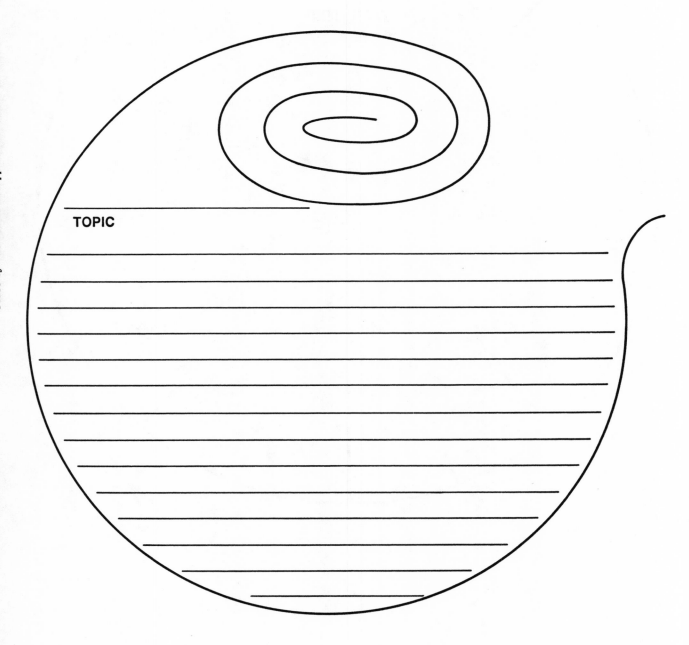

TOPIC

TAKE ACTION

Take a trip to your local airport. Gather brochures from each airline and make notes about all the facilities and services the airport provides for the public.

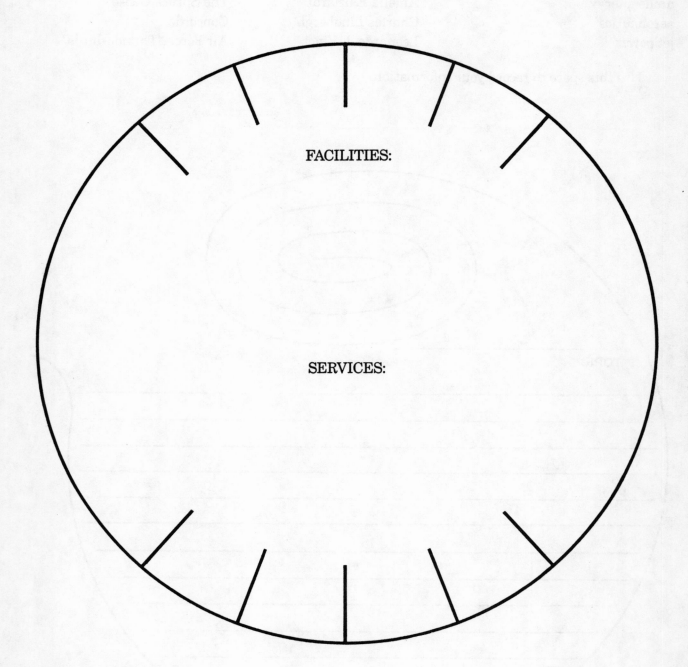

FACILITIES:

SERVICES:

CONTRACT

The countdown begins. You hold your breath as you push the IGNITE button; your rocket LIFTS OFF! Everything is perfect as your model zooms high into the air, then gently parachutes safely back to you. You have just shared the feeling that NASA engineers and specialists have at their launches. Model rocketry is a thrilling and challenging hobby that can be enjoyed at all age levels.

My Target activities will be:

_____

_____

_____

My Spinoffs will be:

_____

_____

_____

I will Take Action by:

_____

_____

_____

My study will begin on _____.

Date

My goal is to finish by _____.

Date

_____
Student Signature

_____
Teacher Signature

TARGET ACTIVITY

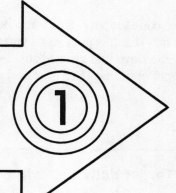

At one time, model rocketry was a very dangerous hobby. Make a poster comparing unsafe methods of the past to the safer measures used today.

Bring the completed poster to a local toy and hobby shop; perhaps they will display it!

(Past):   **Unsafe**

(Today):   **Safe**

TARGET ACTIVITY

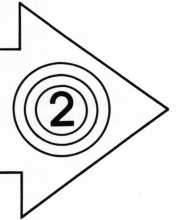

Draw a series of diagrams to compare the design and parts of a model rocket and an actual rocket, such as the *Saturn*.

Model Rocket

Saturn

Mount your diagrams on a poster for classroom display.

TARGET ACTIVITY

Collect and write a list of building and launching success tips. These can be gathered from reading, interviews, and your own experiences.

TIPS:

"Do's"

"Don'ts"

Organize these tips in booklet form and donate it to your school library.

TARGET ACTIVITY

Trace the launch and flight path of a model rocket on the chalkboard, and explain the different phases. Then take the class outside for a real launch—*only after you have received permission from the principal and your teacher!*

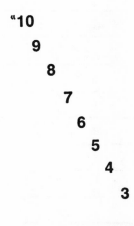

"10
9
8
7
6
5
4
3
2
1"

SPINOFF SELECTIONS

Select one of these topics for further research about model rocketry.

Robert Goddard	parachute	gravity
engine—solid fuel	aerodynamics	drag
ballistics	jet propulsion	perigee/apogee

Use this space to record your information.

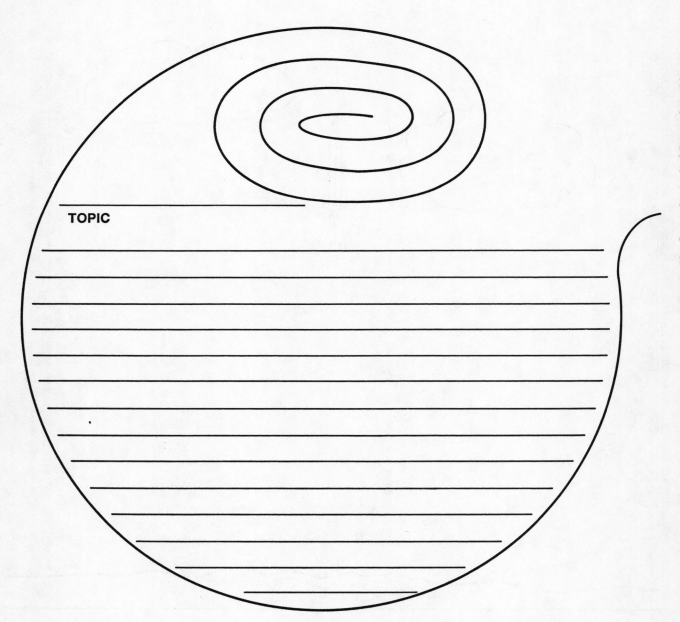

TOPIC

TAKE ACTION

If you would like information about rocket clubs in your area, or other information concerning model rocketry as a hobby, write to the following addresses:

National Association of Rocketry
182 Madison Avenue
Elizabeth, New Jersey 07201

International Civil Aviation Organization
Place de L'Aviation Internationale
1000 Sherbrooke Street West
Montreal, Quebec CANADA H3A 2R2

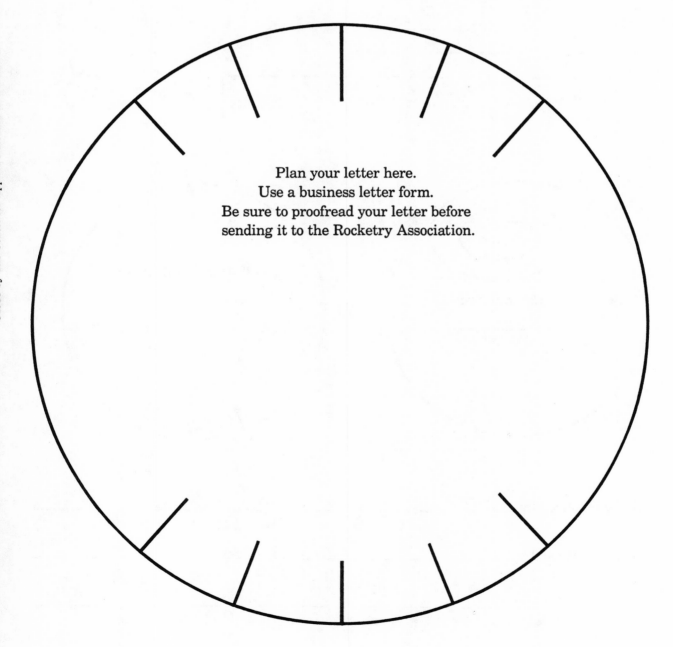

Plan your letter here.
Use a business letter form.
Be sure to proofread your letter before
sending it to the Rocketry Association.

CONTRACT

Captain Nemo of science fiction fame traveled 20,000 leagues under the sea in a submarine named *The Nautilus*. Long before Jules Verne wrote this story, people had been interested in exploring under the sea—even as far back as 333 B.C.! Formerly thought of as a vessel only for wartime use, today's nuclear-powered and mini-subs are carrying out valuable scientific research in our underwater world.

My Target activities will be:

_____
_____
_____

My Spinoffs will be:

_____
_____
_____

I will Take Action by:

_____
_____
_____

My study will begin on _____.
Date

My goal is to finish by _____.
Date

_____   _____
Student Signature   Teacher Signature

TARGET ACTIVITY

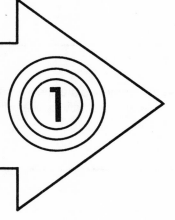

Create an underwater mural that illustrates at least 10 types of submarines, the kinds of work they do, and the depths to which they will submerge.

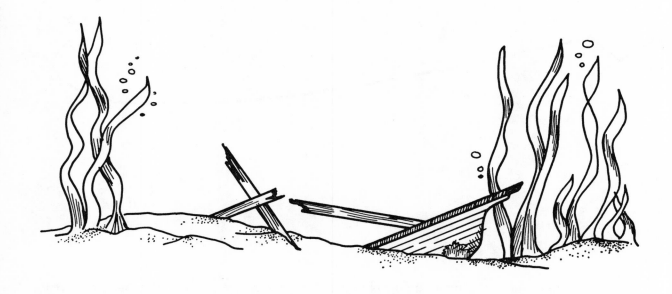

You might like to include submarines from the past in your 10 choices. Look for likenesses and differences in the submarines you choose.

TARGET ACTIVITY

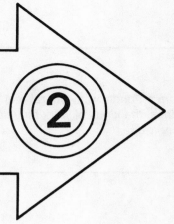

Today's submarines are like a community for the people who serve on them. Make a cutaway diagram illustrating the sections of a modern submarine.

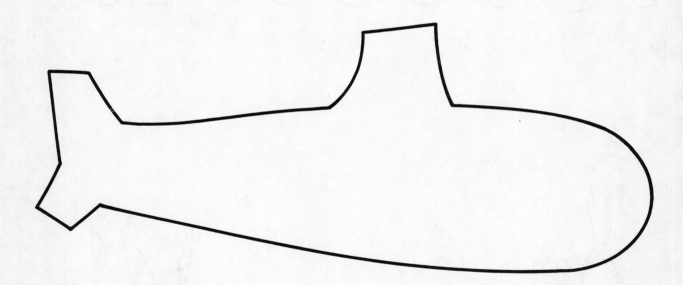

Include dimensions, when possible, as you label your sections. How do these dimensions compare to rooms in your home or school? How many people occupy these spaces at one time? Pretend you are serving aboard this submarine and write some diary entries that describe your days and nights.

TARGET ACTIVITY

The periscope is an optical instrument used to see above the water while submerged to a small depth. Draw a diagram that shows how a periscope works.

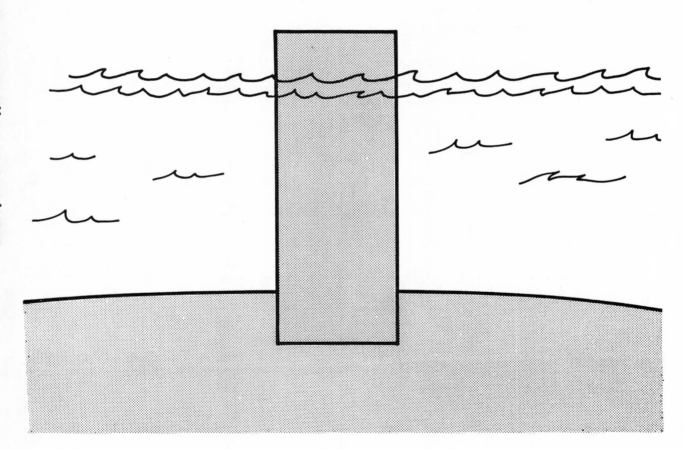

Can you make a working model of a periscope? Use a quart milk carton and some small mirrors. What can you do with your periscope? When would a periscope be useful to have? Demonstrate this model for your class.

TARGET ACTIVITY

A submarine must be made more buoyant for it to rise from deep under the water to the surface of the water. Test at least 20 different objects to determine if they will float. Can you find ways to make the sinkers more buoyant?

OBJECT	BUOYANT Yes	No	BUOYANCY IDEAS FOR SINKERS
1.			
2.			
3.			
4.			
5.			
6.			
7.			
8.			
9.			
10.			
11.			
12.			
13.			
14.			
15.			

Read about the actual methods used to raise a submarine through the ocean depths. Plan an experiment to show your class how this is done.

SPINOFF SELECTIONS

Select one of these topics for further research about submarines.

sonar	*Monitor/Merrimac*	Jacques Cousteau	Edward Beach
radar	bathysphere	August Piccard	Robert Fulton
water pressure	*USS Triton*	Simon Lake	M. d'Equevilley
submersible	U-boat	John Holland	Jules Verne

Use this space to record your information.

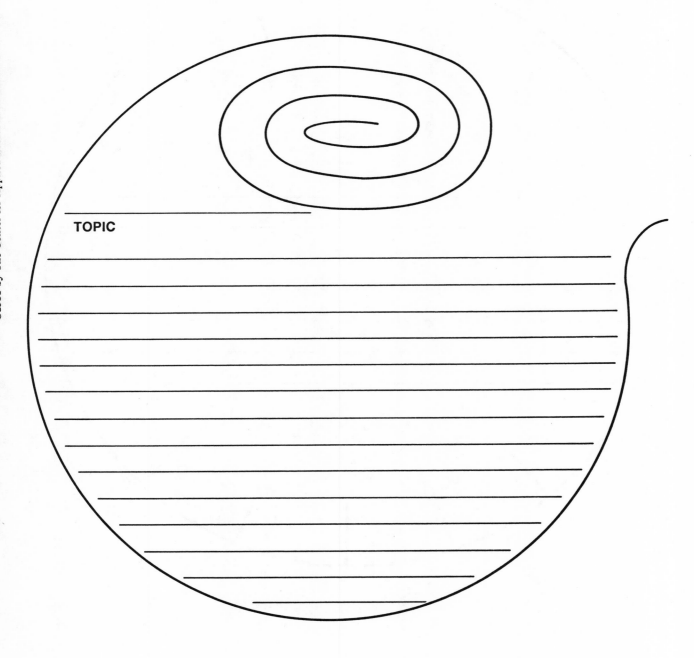

TOPIC

TAKE ACTION

Invite a person who has served on a submarine to speak to your class about life aboard this type of vessel. To identify a person, you might: (1) ask your teacher to contact the volunteer speaker's bureau for your district, or (2) call the local Navy Recruiting Station and ask them for help.

Use the space below for questions you would like to ask your guest. (Be sure to get the speaker's address and write a thank-you note!)

CONTRACT

Who or what is really out there? We have always wondered about space and the tiny specks of light beyond our moon and sun. Now that we are able to send probes into space and view them through cameras, the eyes of astronauts, and radio signals, our knowledge is growing. We who are land-based continue to magnify our vision by looking through telescopes.

My Target activities will be:

_____

_____

_____

My Spinoffs will be:

_____

_____

_____

I will Take Action by:

_____

_____

My study will begin on _____.

Date

My goal is to finish by _____.

Date

_____   _____
Student Signature   Teacher Signature

TARGET ACTIVITY

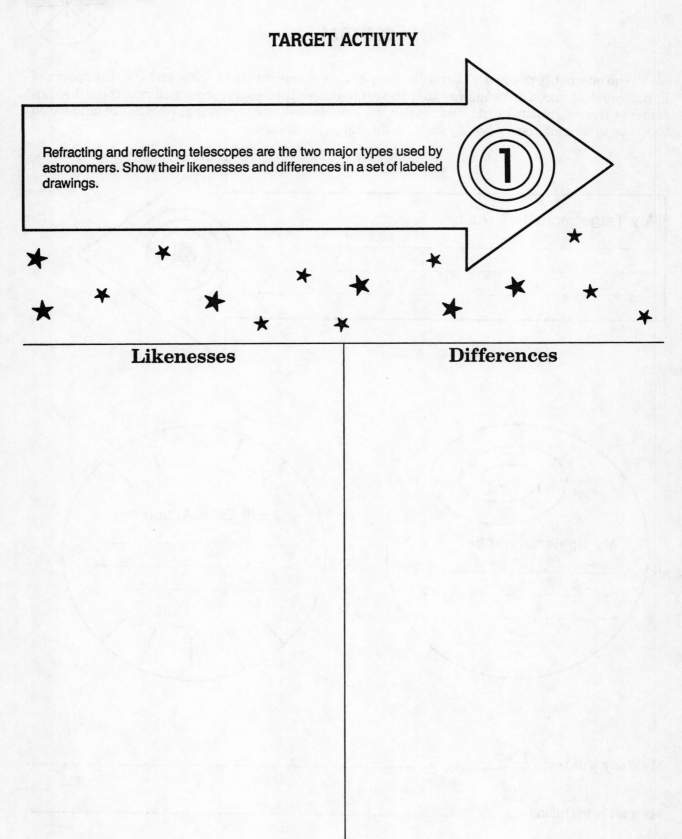

Refracting and reflecting telescopes are the two major types used by astronomers. Show their likenesses and differences in a set of labeled drawings.

①

Likenesses	Differences

Examine kinds of telescopes found in hobby shops and department stores in your area.

TARGET ACTIVITY

Do some reading and make a calendar of Astronomical Events to observe through a telescope during the year. You might include a "stars of the seasons" section! What would be some viewing tips to keep in mind? Add these facts and illustrations to your calendar.

February

January

March

May

April

June

August

September

July

November

October

December

TARGET ACTIVITY

Write a story as if you are the telescope at a famous observatory. Name the observatory and include real events that have been viewed through "you"!

③

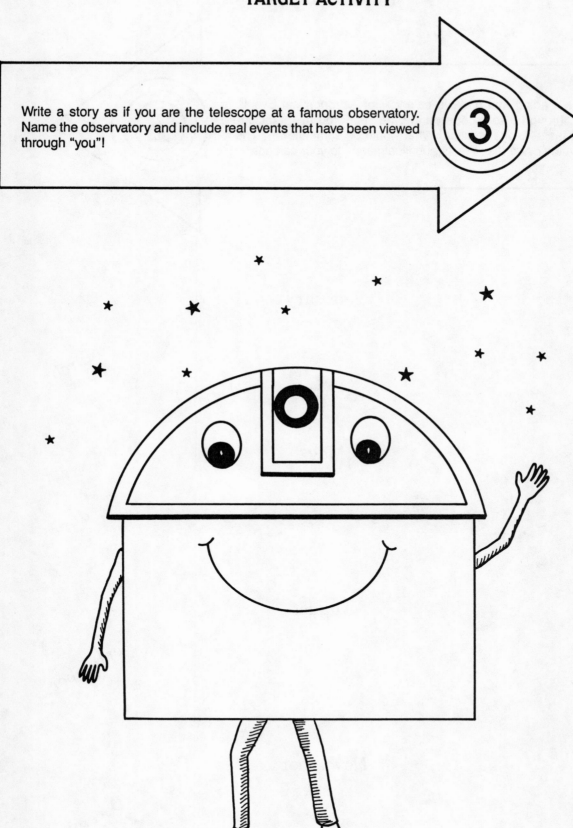

TARGET ACTIVITY

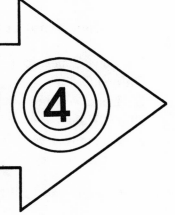

Space distances are so vast that scientists had to develop new measurement units to record them. Make a mobile illustrating one of these units.

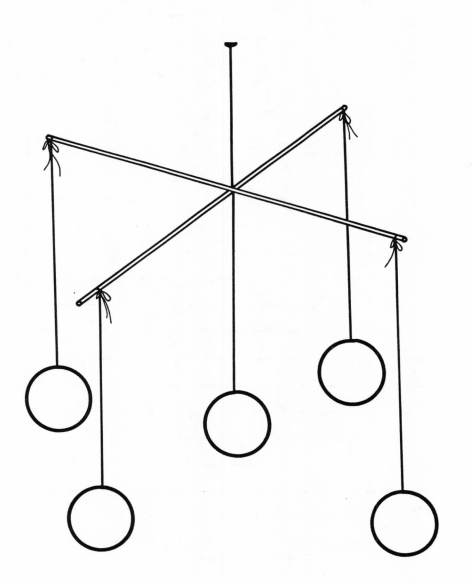

SPINOFF SELECTIONS

Select one of these topics for further research about telescopes.

Nicolaus Copernicus	radio telescope	moon
Galileo Galilei	Mount Wilson Observatory	lens
Sir Isaac Newton	Mount Palomar Observatory	constellations
Ellery Hale	Lick Observatory	comets
refracting telescope	Yerkes Observatory	galaxies
reflecting telescope	stars	planets

Use this space to record your information.

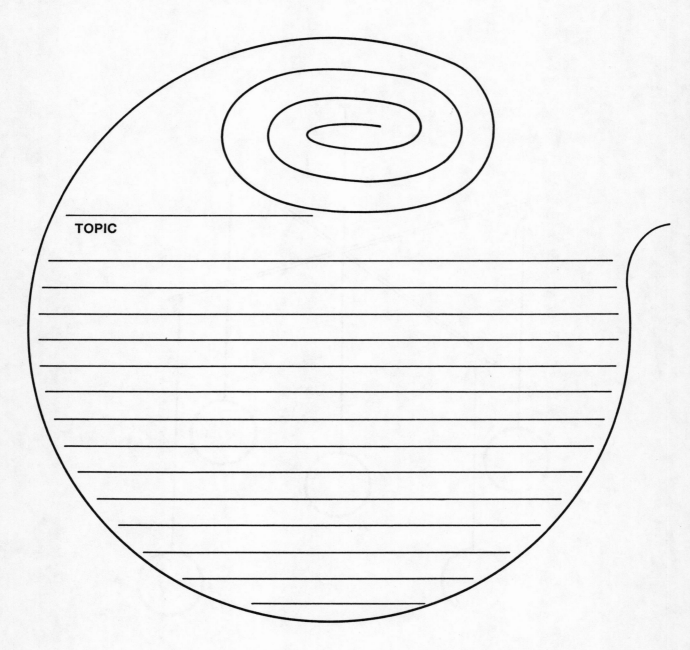

TOPIC

TAKE ACTION

If there is an observatory or planetarium in your community, call to arrange a field trip for yourself!

OR

Begin an astronomy club and invite friends to join who have telescopes or an interest in this topic. Plan some night sky viewings. Invite your parents for some of these events.

Use the planning sheet for the Take Action activity you choose.

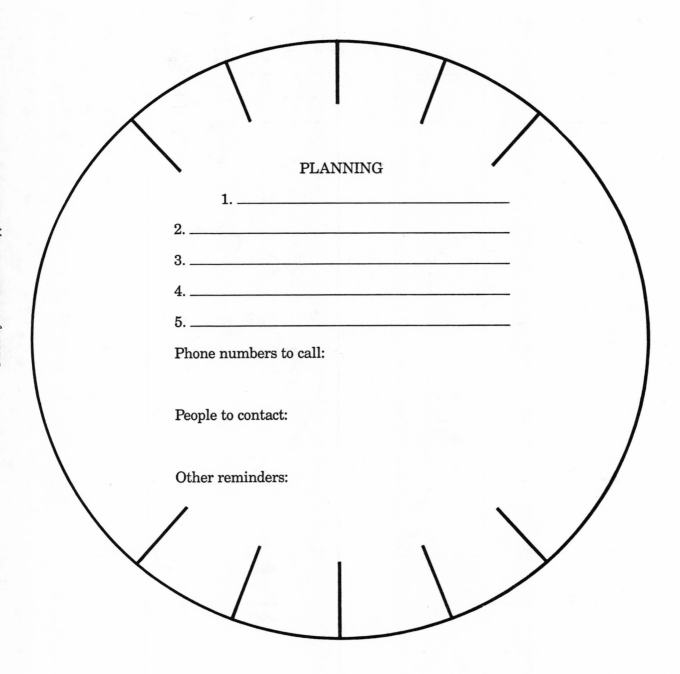

PLANNING

1. _____

2. _____

3. _____

4. _____

5. _____

Phone numbers to call:

People to contact:

Other reminders:

CONTRACT

The year 2000 is almost here! What will the world be like? People who are interested in studying about the future are called futurists. They examine trends of current happenings and make predictions based on these trends. Present technology and needs people have are taken into consideration when futurists look ahead and try to analyze and describe future outcomes. You will take a step towards becoming a futurist after completing these activities.

My Target activities will be:

_____

_____

_____

My Spinoffs will be:

_____

_____

_____

I will Take Action by:

_____

_____

_____

My study will begin on _____.

Date

My goal is to finish by _____.

Date

_____   _____
Student Signature   Teacher Signature

TARGET ACTIVITY

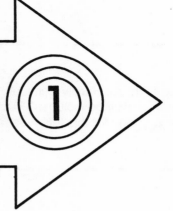

Someday we might have the capability to colonize and live on another planet! In order to accomplish this task, necessities sustaining human life will have to be provided. If the planet to be settled is Jupiter, describe the special considerations needed for food, clothing, and shelter.

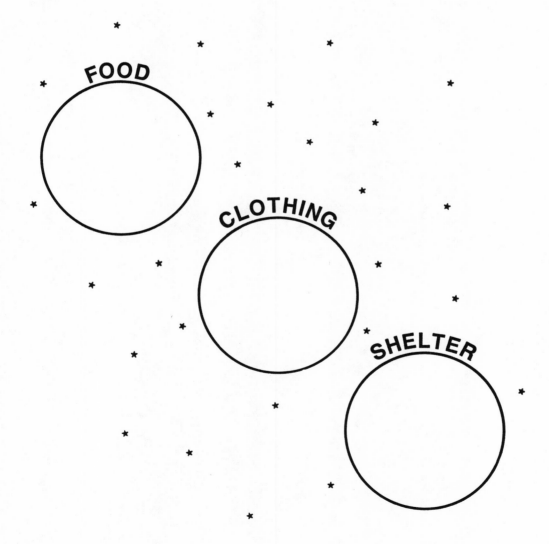

Construct a diorama of the colony for display including features from each category above.

TARGET ACTIVITY

What might the family car look like in the year 2020? What new innovations will be included? What would its power source contain? Draw a design for this future car and label the new features.

Future Car Planning Sheet

Give this future car a name and create an advertisement to sell the new design. How much should it cost?

TARGET ACTIVITY

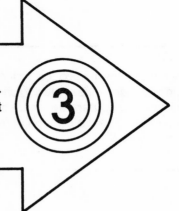

Many new applications developed for the space program have become part of our lives, such as freeze-dried foods and velcro tabs. List others and explain ways each might be used in the year 2020.

ITEM   **USE**

_____   _____
_____   _____
_____   _____
_____   _____
_____   _____
_____   _____
_____   _____
_____   _____
_____   _____
_____   _____
_____   _____
_____   _____
_____   _____
_____   _____

Which idea is the most practical? Why?

TARGET ACTIVITY

Solving problems in seconds, storing thousands of bits of information, drawing, creating music, playing chess, diagnosing illnesses—will the wonders of computers ever cease? New adaptations are being developed daily. Draw a cartoon showing a new task computers could perform for you!

CAPTION:

SPINOFF SELECTIONS

Select one of these topics for further research about the future.

NASA   planets   future housing
space shuttle   black holes   future transportations
Mariner and space probes   robotics   space exploration
computers   astronomy   futurists
ocean farming   future foods

Use this space to record your information.

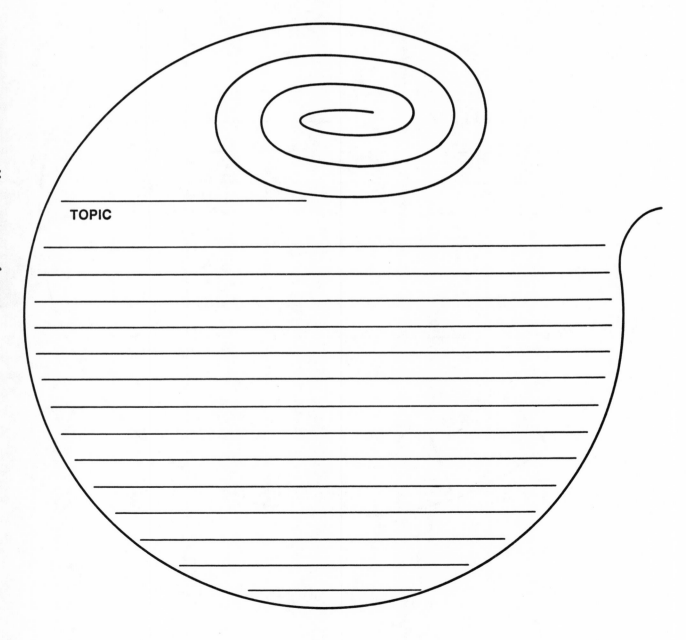

TOPIC

TAKE ACTION

Present a speech to classmates convincing them of the importance for continued space exploration. List important points to be made. Prepare note cards for your speech.

Use the form below to plan your Take Action activity.

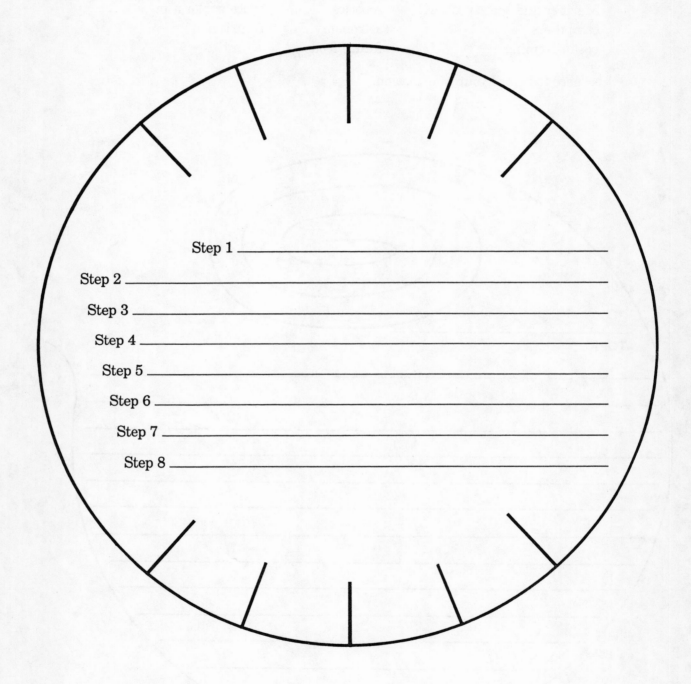

Step 1 _____

Step 2 _____

Step 3 _____

Step 4 _____

Step 5 _____

Step 6 _____

Step 7 _____

Step 8 _____

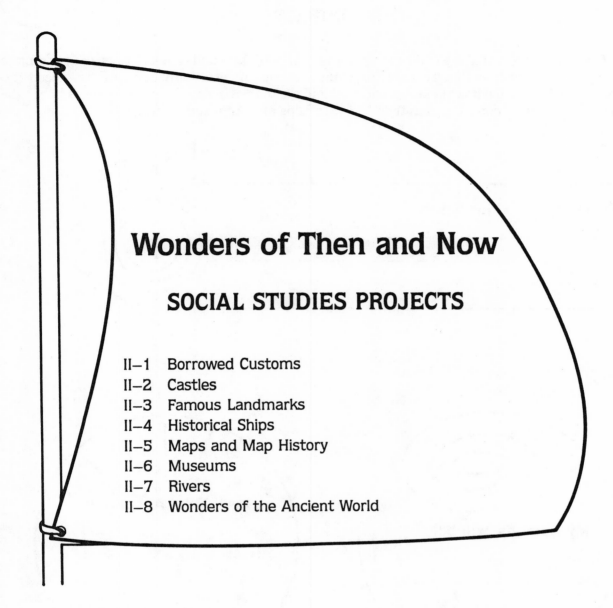

Wonders of Then and Now

SOCIAL STUDIES PROJECTS

II–1 Borrowed Customs
II–2 Castles
II–3 Famous Landmarks
II–4 Historical Ships
II–5 Maps and Map History
II–6 Museums
II–7 Rivers
II–8 Wonders of the Ancient World

CONTRACT

Our country is a mixture of people from a variety of backgrounds and cultures, each adding to our way of life. The "great melting pot" or a "tapestry woven from many cultures" have been two phrases used to describe this blend of people that make up our citizenry. Whether in the past or in the present, immigrants enter our country filled with hope and enthusiasm for a new way of life.

My Target activities will be:

_____
_____
_____

My Spinoffs will be:

_____
_____
_____

I will Take Action by:

_____
_____
_____

My study will begin on _____.
Date

My goal is to finish by _____.
Date

_____   _____
Student Signature   Teacher Signature

TARGET ACTIVITY

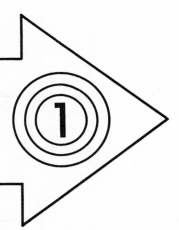

Set up a cultural glossary that describes some customs borrowed from other countries and their origins. Use the categories listed below to organize the information.

TOYS AND GAMES	FOODS	CLOTHING	VOCABULARY WORDS

CELEBRATIONS/ HOLIDAYS	PLACE NAMES (Cities, Rivers, Mountains)	SAYINGS	ARCHITECTURE

Create a scrapbook display to share the glossary. Include pictures from magazines or newspapers, photographs, drawings, or real items to make the display more interesting.

TARGET ACTIVITY

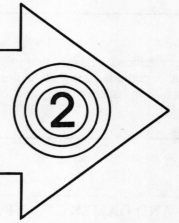

Explain in an essay the advantages we have had in being a "great melting pot" or a "tapestry woven from many cultures." What can we each gain in a personal way from another culture?

TARGET ACTIVITY

Learn some basic words and phrases from three other languages. Look for similarities among the languages in pronunciation and spelling. (Greetings, numbers from one to ten, and everyday items are examples of basic categories to investigate.)

ENGLISH WORD/PHRASE	———— LANGUAGE	———— LANGUAGE	———— LANGUAGE

Requiring new citizens to learn and speak English has been a matter of debate recently. What is your opinion on this matter? Discuss this topic with other classmates.

TARGET ACTIVITY

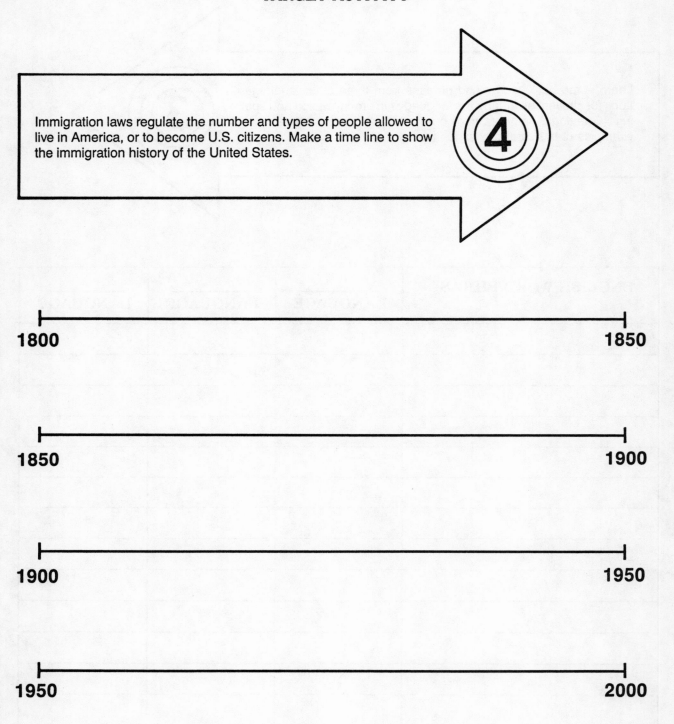

Immigration laws regulate the number and types of people allowed to live in America, or to become U.S. citizens. Make a time line to show the immigration history of the United States.

4

1800 — 1850

1850 — 1900

1900 — 1950

1950 — 2000

Identify 10 famous people who were immigrants to the United States in this century. List their contributions to all Americans.

SPINOFF SELECTIONS

Select one of these topics for further research about borrowed customs.

immigration laws	Mardi Gras	karate/judo
naturalization laws	language origins	plaids
Ellis Island	American Indians	soccer
pita bread	soufflé	jai alai

Use this space to record your information.

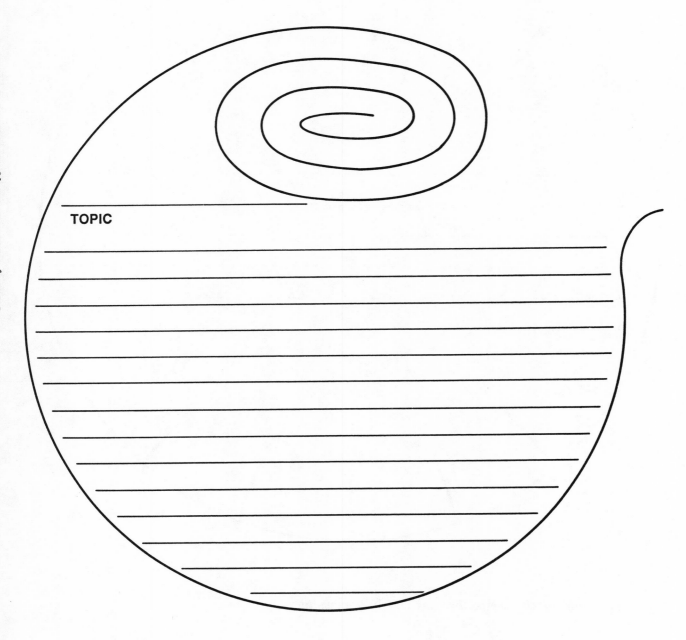

TOPIC

TAKE ACTION

Visit a chef in a local restaurant specializing in ethnic foods. Ask the chef to describe cooking techniques, recipes, and ingredients used in this type of food. Perhaps the chef will give you his or her favorite recipe! If you cannot make a visit, look in cookbooks for an interesting recipe or watch a culinary television show.

Use the form below to list questions to ask or to record the recipe.

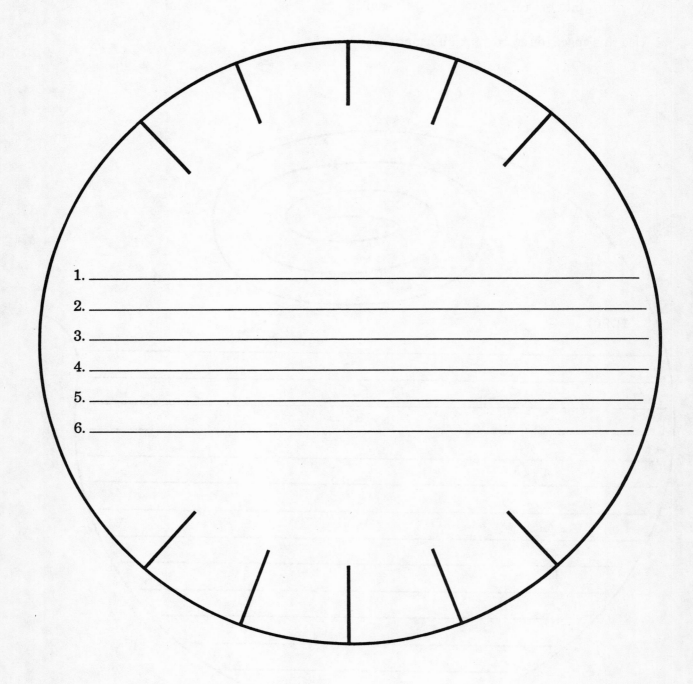

1. _____

2. _____

3. _____

4. _____

5. _____

6. _____

Try preparing the recipe for your family or classmates.

CONTRACT

"Once upon a time, there lived in a castle"…

　　Castles were both homes and fortresses for ruling kings and the rich and powerful. They were centers of commerce, government, the military, and society in general. Many were built with secret rooms, dungeons, towers, and moats. Although many are now uninhabited, they are a spectacular sight for tourists from all over the world.

My Target activities will be:

_____
_____
_____

My Spinoffs will be:

_____
_____
_____

I will Take Action by:

_____
_____
_____

My study will begin on _____.
　　　　　　　　　　　　　　　　Date

My goal is to finish by _____.
　　　　　　　　　　　　　　　　Date

_____　　_____
　　　　Student Signature　　　　　　　　Teacher Signature

TARGET ACTIVITY

Make a list of features that were commonly found in castles. Draw a castle floor plan that combines many of these features.

1

FEATURES: _____

_____

_____

_____

FLOOR PLAN:

Which features are used in many homes today? Can you find pictures to show the transition from castle to home?

TARGET ACTIVITY

Pretend that you are a real estate agent who has the listing for a castle. Select the castle and create an advertisement that will both inform and entice a prospective buyer.

TARGET ACTIVITY

Research two famous castles and point out the likenesses and differences in an oral talk. Use the form below to record information.

③

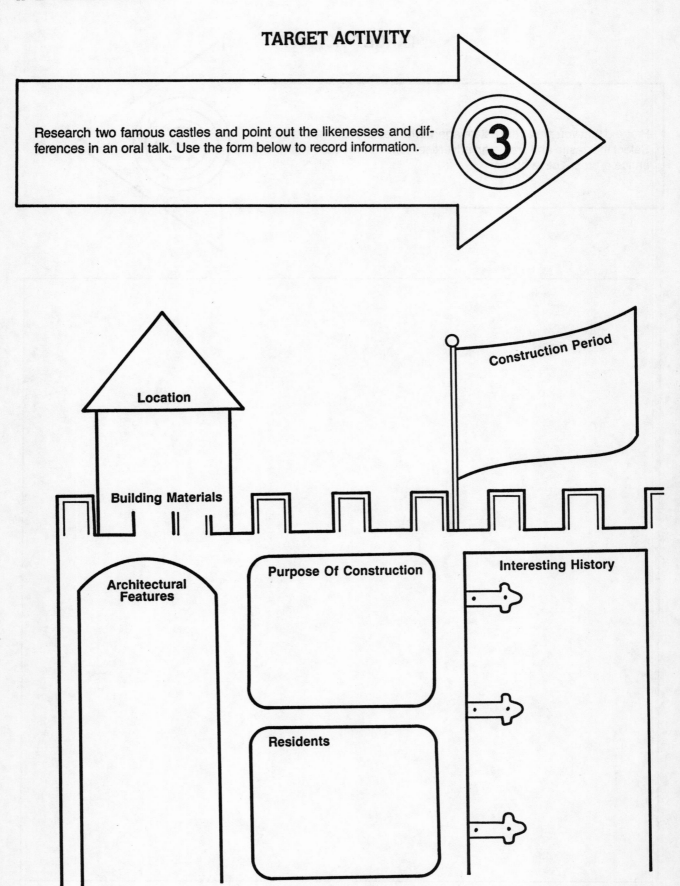

Location

Construction Period

Building Materials

Architectural Features

Purpose Of Construction

Interesting History

Residents

TARGET ACTIVITY

Castles were the forerunners of modern day forts. Compare the defense techniques used in many castles and forts throughout history.

GEOGRAPHIC LOCATIONS

Castle	Fort

CONSTRUCTION METHODS

Castle	Fort

PROTECTIVE DEVICES FOR PEOPLE

Castle	Fort

BUILDING MATERIALS

Castle	Fort

Draw or collect pictures of weapons and methods used by medieval soldiers when attacking or defending a castle.

SPINOFF SELECTIONS

Select one of these topics for further research about castles.

medieval life	knights	heraldry	madrigals
feudal system	King Arthur	guilds	kings and queens
famous castles	Camelot	great hall	fairy tales
court jester	Neuschwanstein	clothes	

Use this space to record your information.

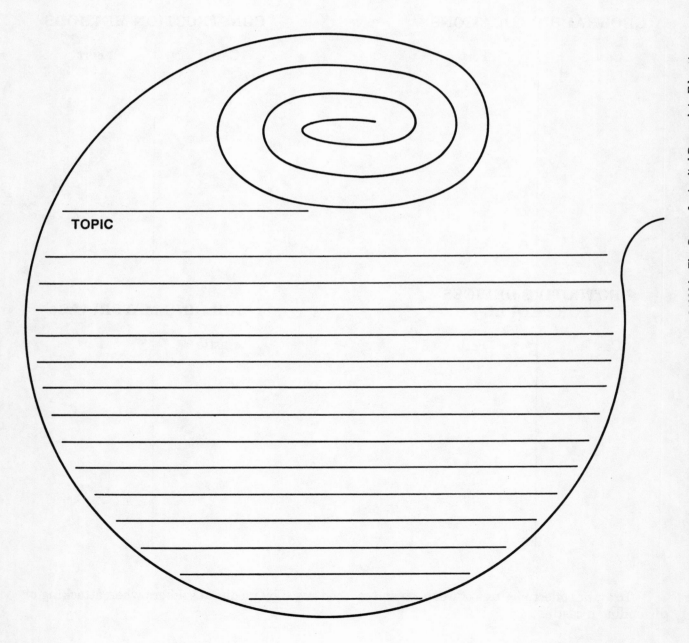

TOPIC

TAKE ACTION

Build a castle model of historic or original design. Use the checklist below as a guide.

☐ Draw a building plan.
☐ Collect building materials. (Cardboard boxes and tubes work well.)
☐ Construct the castle.
☐ Label each room and special area.
☐ Create a family history for the imaginary residents.
  Include titles, names, deeds, interests, and the like.
☐ Design a flag to be used when the family is in residence.
☐ Design a coat of arms for the imaginary family.
☐ Ask permission to display your model in the library.
☐ Gather informative reading material about the medieval era,
  to be used along with the display.

CONTRACT

When a friend goes on vacation and sends you a postcard, the picture will probably be a famous landmark of that area. Throughout the world there are statues, buildings, towers, cathedrals, museums, temples, and monuments that are "musts" to see when you visit a city or country. These landmarks are symbols of pride and remembrance for many people.

My Target activities will be:

_____

_____

_____

My Spinoffs will be:

_____

_____

_____

I will Take Action by:

_____

_____

_____

My study will begin on _____.

Date

My goal is to finish by _____.

Date

_____   _____
Student Signature   Teacher Signature

TARGET ACTIVITY

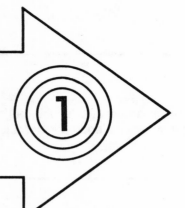

Choose a country and identify three well-known landmarks found there. Use the headings below to organize research about the landmarks, and then design a souvenir postcard for each of the three.

Souvenir Postcard of _____

LOCATION

IMPORTANT YEARS IN HISTORY
(Dedication, Events, Construction)

IMPORTANT PEOPLE
(Founder, Builder,
Originator)

SYMBOLISM REPRESENTED

NUMBERS OF PEOPLE VISITING EACH YEAR

MANNER IN WHICH IT ACHIEVED IMPORTANCE

PURPOSE OF ORIGINAL DESIGN

CHANGES/RENOVATIONS OVER THE YEARS

Use the three squares above to design an appropriate stamp for each postcard.

TARGET ACTIVITY

Explain in an essay why you feel that citizens of all nations should preserve famous landmarks for future generations.

②

ESSAY OUTLINE

I. _____

  A. _____

  B. _____

  C. _____

II. _____

  A. _____

  B. _____

  C. _____

III. _____

  A. _____

  B. _____

  C. _____

Send your essay to the editor of the local and/or school newspaper.

TARGET ACTIVITY

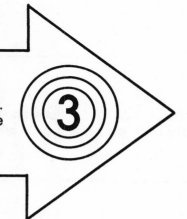

Select a type of landmark such as those mentioned on the contract. Choose 5 to 10 examples of this type. Follow the steps below to create a silhouette of each.

1. Landmark type: _____

2. International examples: _____

   _____

   _____

3. Measurements/dimensions:

   _____

   _____

   _____

   _____

   _____

   _____

   _____

   _____

   _____

4. Make a scale drawing of the front view of each landmark. Use a reasonable number of inches to each foot so that the shape will be recognizable.

5. Trace the scale drawing on black paper or poster board and cut out the drawing.

6. Ask classmates to identify each of the silhouettes. Use the silhouettes as a mobile or bulletin board display.

TARGET ACTIVITY

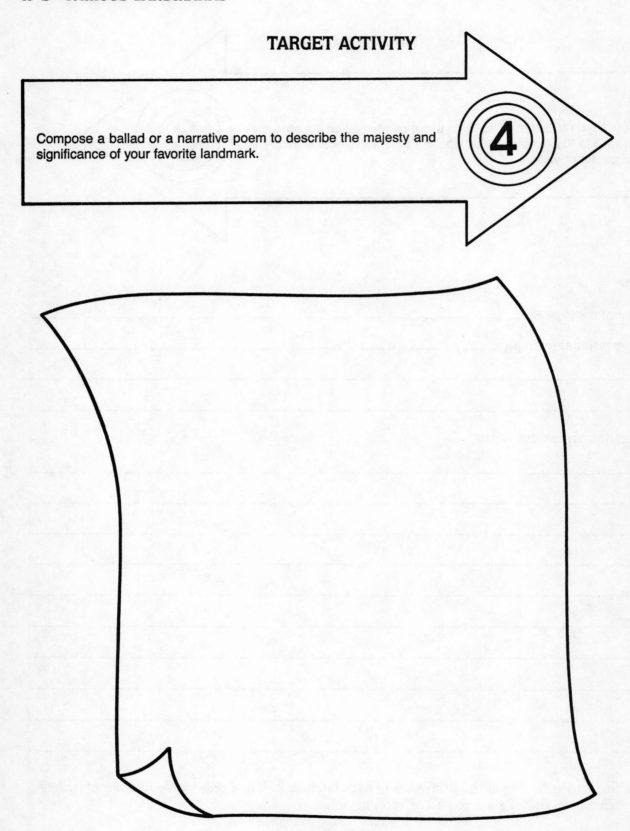

Compose a ballad or a narrative poem to describe the majesty and significance of your favorite landmark.

④

Send your original composition to the embassy for that country, or to appropriate government officials. Ask librarians or teachers for assistance with addresses.

SPINOFF SELECTIONS

Select one of these topics for further research about famous landmarks.

Statue of Liberty	The Parthenon	Lincoln Memorial
Washington Monument	The Colosseum	Great Wall of China
Arc de Triomphe	Taj Mahal	Temple of Angkor Wat
Notre Dame Cathedral	Eiffel Tower	Pyramids
Independence Hall	Big Ben	Royal Canadian Mounted
C. N. Tower	Leaning Tower of Pisa	Police Headquarters

Use this space to record your information.

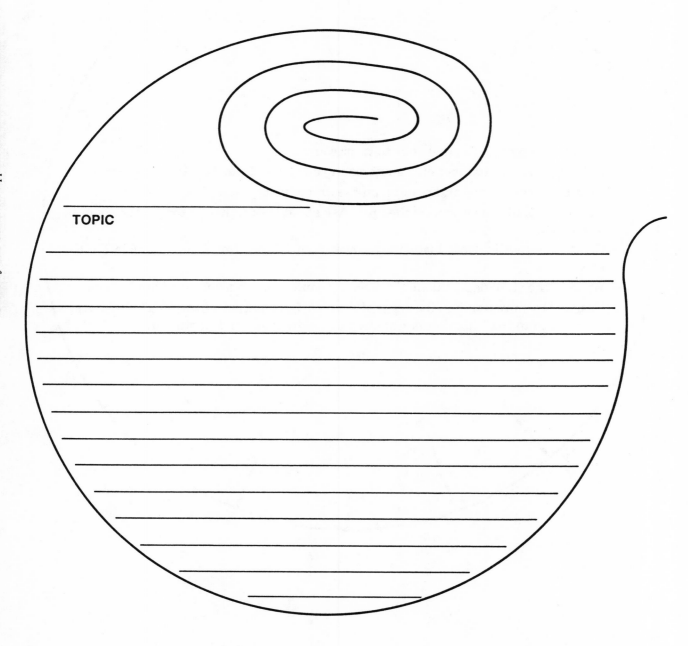

TOPIC

TAKE ACTION

What landmark in your town or county should a tourist be sure to visit? Do you know its history? Is it in good repair, or is there a need for restoration? Find out about local historic sites in one or more of the following ways.

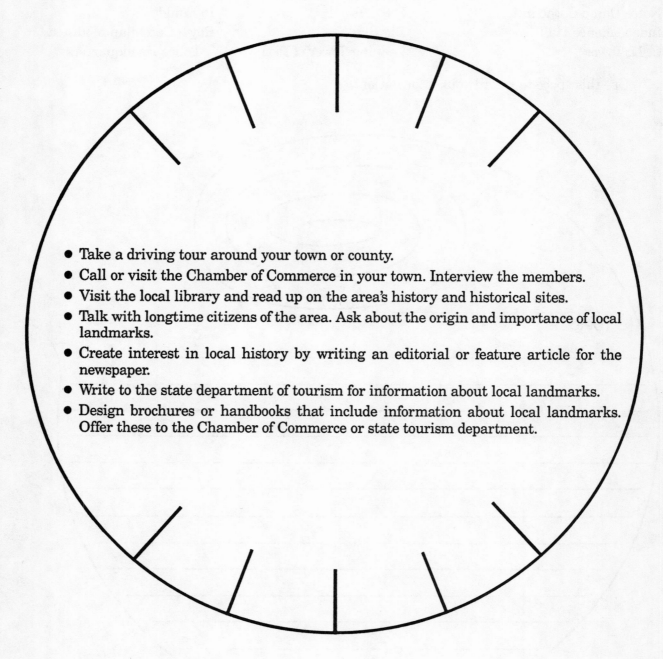

- Take a driving tour around your town or county.
- Call or visit the Chamber of Commerce in your town. Interview the members.
- Visit the local library and read up on the area's history and historical sites.
- Talk with longtime citizens of the area. Ask about the origin and importance of local landmarks.
- Create interest in local history by writing an editorial or feature article for the newspaper.
- Write to the state department of tourism for information about local landmarks.
- Design brochures or handbooks that include information about local landmarks. Offer these to the Chamber of Commerce or state tourism department.

CONTRACT

Trim the mizzenmasts…heave, ho, laddies…aweigh anchors! Seafaring terms such as these are unique and colorful. They remind us of many ships that have taken an important place in history. Each ship has a special character created from its individual design, purpose, and history. Looking at their pictures stimulates our imaginations and calls to mind adventures and times of an era long ago.

My Target activities will be:

_____
_____
_____

My Spinoffs will be:

_____
_____
_____

I will Take Action by:

_____
_____
_____

My study will begin on _____.

Date

My goal is to finish by _____.

Date

_____   _____
Student Signature   Teacher Signature

TARGET ACTIVITY

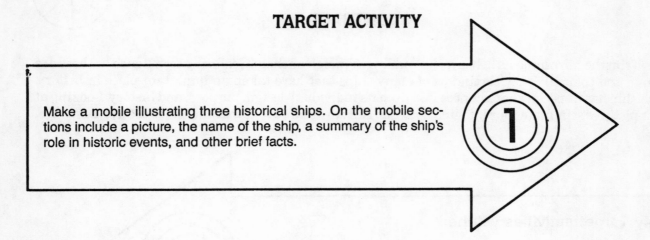

Make a mobile illustrating three historical ships. On the mobile sections include a picture, the name of the ship, a summary of the ship's role in historic events, and other brief facts.

Duplicate three of these forms to use in recording your research about each ship.

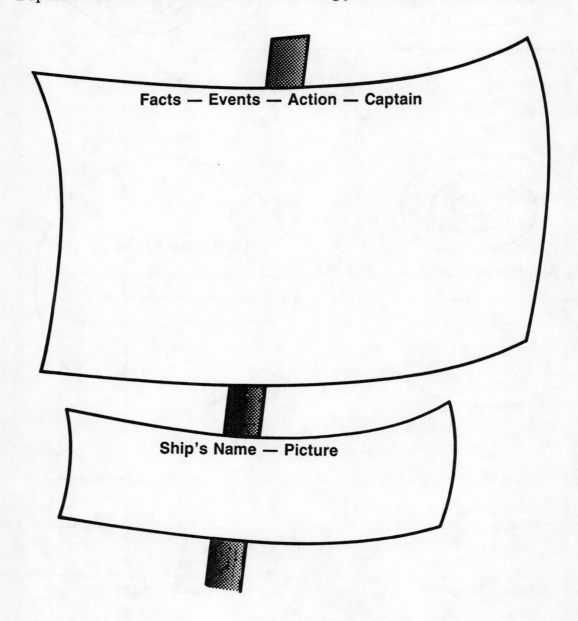

Facts — Events — Action — Captain

Ship's Name — Picture

TARGET ACTIVITY

Choose a famous ship and imagine yourself aboard as a crew member. Write a poem or song about your life at sea.

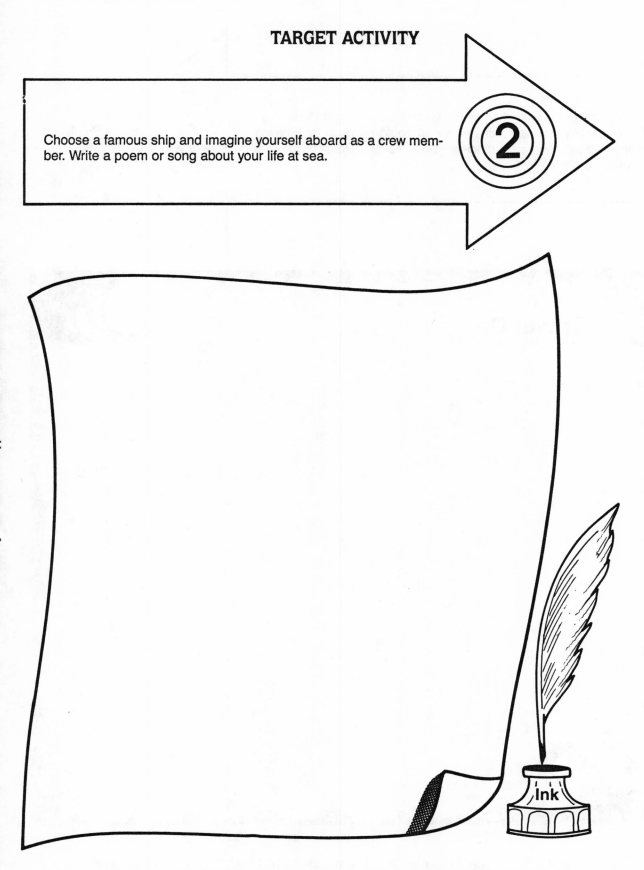

Pretend to be the captain of the ship and make several log entries about your travel.

TARGET ACTIVITY

Choose one of the fastest and most luxurious passenger ships since the 1400s. Write an advertisement that could be used to inform a prospective passenger about speed, price, accommodations, special activities, and the like.

Travel On

Can you locate an example of an original advertisement for that passenger ship or one of its type? If so, compare the two ads for likenesses and differences in style and information.

TARGET ACTIVITY

Many days were very boring and routine on early sailing ships. Sailors turned to activities such as carving scrimshaw, knot tying, needlework, and singing sea chanteys. Research a pastime and share the facts in an oral talk.

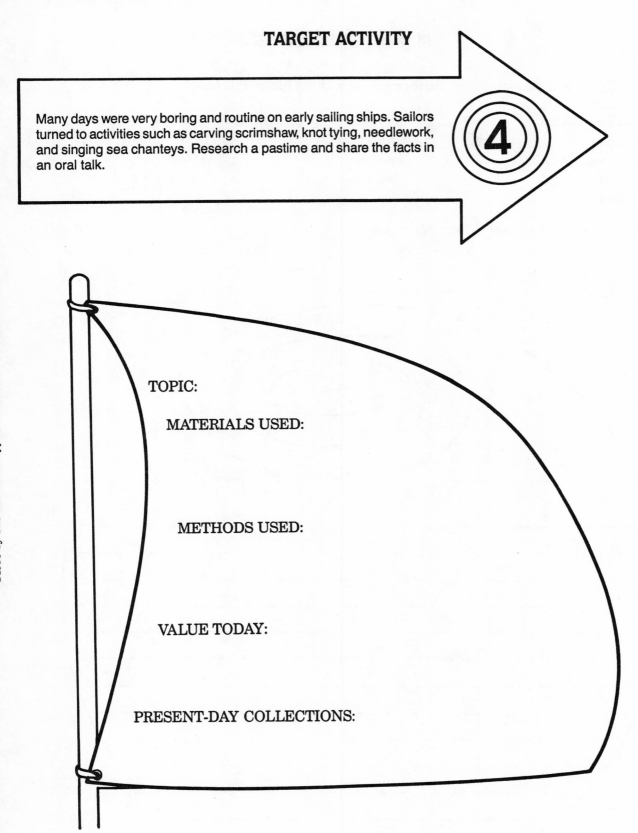

TOPIC:

MATERIALS USED:

METHODS USED:

VALUE TODAY:

PRESENT-DAY COLLECTIONS:

Try your hand at one of these pastimes. Include a demonstration in the oral talk.

SPINOFF SELECTIONS

Select one of these topics for further research about historical ships.

Spanish Armada	*Mayflower*	tall ships
Lusitania	*Old Ironsides*	clipper ships
Monitor and Merrimac	*Titanic*	Vikings
Golden Hind	*Kon-Tiki*	America's Cup Race
Blue Nose		

Use this space to record your information.

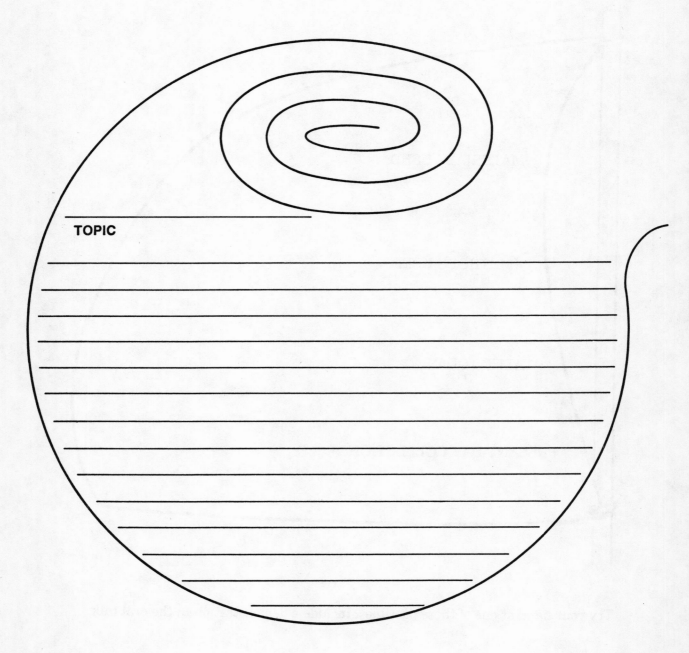

TOPIC

TAKE ACTION

Write a letter to the United States Maritime Agency, Washington, D.C. 10012, and request free educational materials. Make a display for the classroom or library when the materials arrive in the mail. (Hint: Practice writing your letter in the space below; then copy it on school stationery.)

CONTRACT

Our curiosity has always served as a challenge to explore and chart the secrets of the earth's most remote places. Maps have been set down on stone, animal skin, papyrus, and parchment. As we complete the mapping of our own planet, we are now ready to reach out to explore and map other planets, locate distant galaxies, and travel beyond the reaches of our universe.

My Target activities will be:

_____

_____

_____

My Spinoffs will be:

_____

_____

_____

I will Take Action by:

_____

_____

_____

My study will begin on _____.
                                                        Date

My goal is to finish by _____.
                                                        Date

_____   _____
Student Signature   Teacher Signature

©1988 by The Center for Applied Research in Education

TARGET ACTIVITY

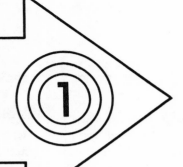

As each early explorer sailed forth to unknown waters and regions of the world, new charts and maps were brought back. Make a crossword puzzle using the names of 18 explorers and the voyages or places they explored.

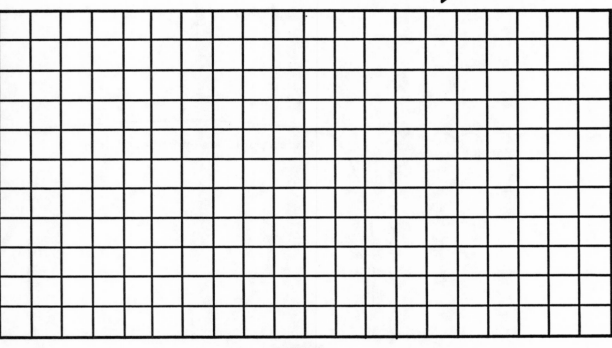

CLUES

Down   Across

_____   _____

_____   _____

_____   _____

_____   _____

_____   _____

_____   _____

_____   _____

_____   _____

TARGET ACTIVITY

Present an informative talk comparing maps of different kinds and regions. *National Geographic Magazine* would be a good source for examples of maps that chart oceans, lands on Earth and in space, as well as space itself.

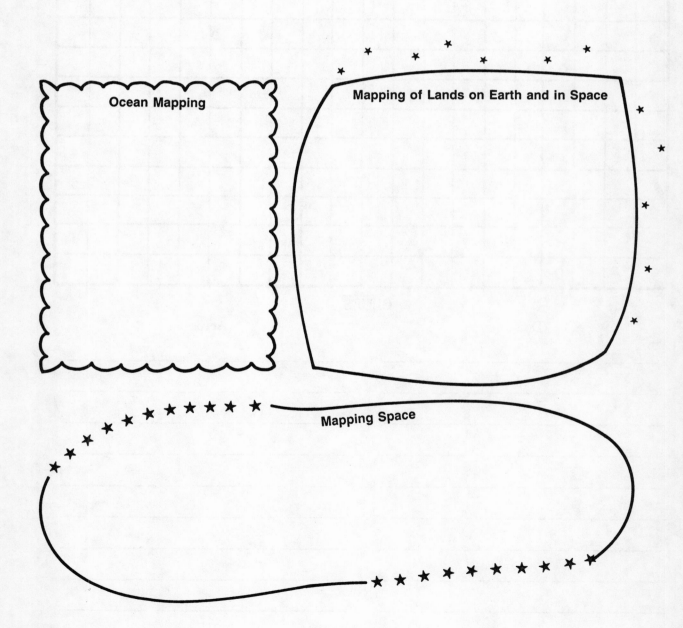

Ocean Mapping

Mapping of Lands on Earth and in Space

Mapping Space

TARGET ACTIVITY

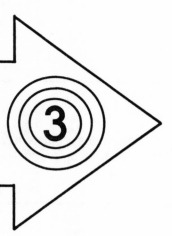

Locate historical maps that show changes as more exploration was completed. Plan a lesson to teach a small group of classmates about these changes and explorations.

Purpose of the Lesson:_____

_____

Vocabulary:_____

_____

References:_____

_____

_____

Steps to Follow:

1. _____

2. _____

3. _____

4. _____

5. _____

6. _____

Estimated Time:_____

   Many ancient maps were made by showing land that the map makers thought were in certain locations. A very early map that astonished modern map makers was the Piri Reis map. See what you can find out about it and use this information in your lesson plan above.

TARGET ACTIVITY

Search for the names of different types of maps so you can make an A, B, C, list of these. Some suggestions are given to help you get started.

A _____

B _____

C _____Celestial Map_____

D _____

E _____

F _____

G _____

H _Hurricane Tracking Map_

I _____

J _____

K _____

L _____

M _____

N _____

O _____

P _____

Q _____

R _____

S _____

T _____Treasure Map_____

U _____

V _____

W _____

X _____

Y _____

Z _____

You may find more than one name for some letters. Have a contest and see who can locate the most types and varieties.

SPINOFF SELECTIONS

Select one of these topics for further research about maps and map history.

The Catalan Charts	navigation	Magellan
windrose charts	cartography	Marco Polo
cuneiform texts	surveying	Thor Heyerdahl
celestial navigation	Prince Henry	National Aeronautics
Samuel de Champlain	John Cabot	and Space Administration

Use this space to record your information.

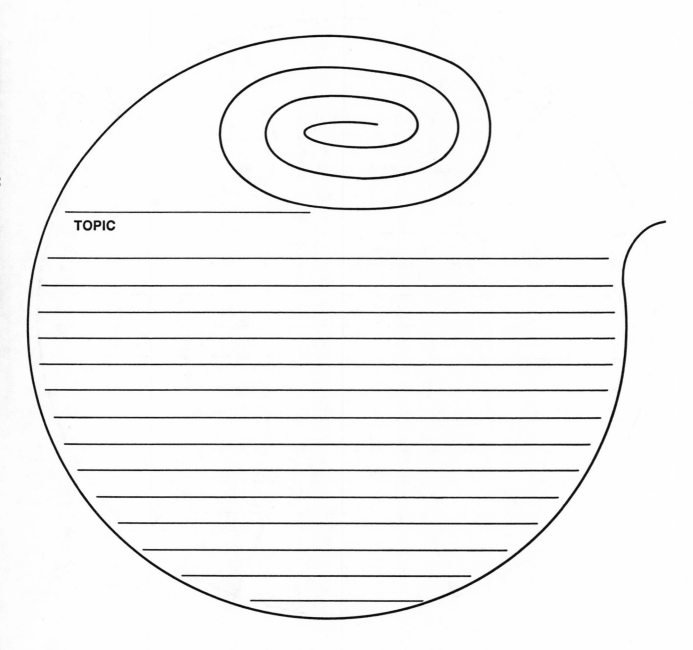

TOPIC

TAKE ACTION

What training must you have to be a cartographer or map maker? What instruments are used to draw maps?

To find the answers to these and other questions you may have about this topic, write a letter to the following address:

American Cartographic Association
c/o American Congress on Surveying and Mapping
210 Little Falls Street
Falls Church, Virginia 22046

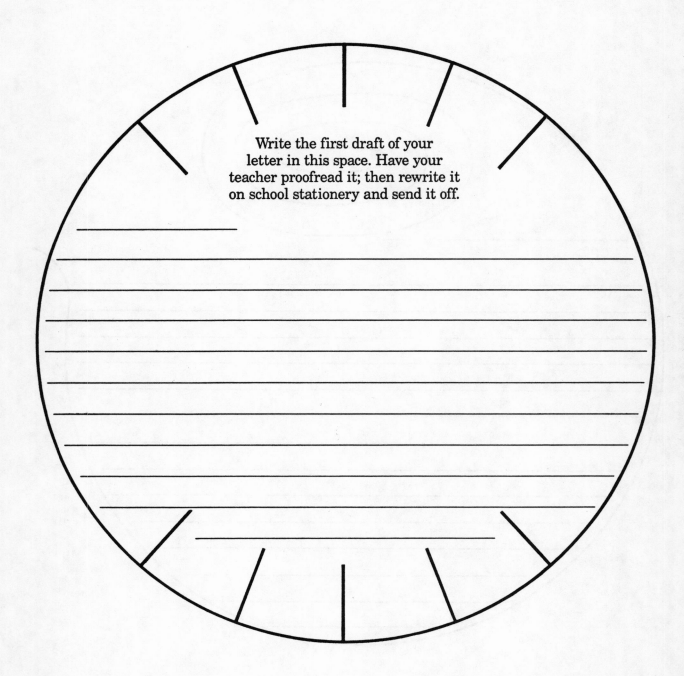

Write the first draft of your letter in this space. Have your teacher proofread it; then rewrite it on school stationery and send it off.

CONTRACT

A collector's dream—art, history, natural history, science and technology, transportation, drama, sports—all represented in museums throughout the world. The Louvre in Paris, France, and the Smithsonian in Washington, D.C., are just two of the great storehouses of memorabilia and knowledge that can be visited.

My Target activities will be:

_____

_____

_____

My Spinoffs will be:

_____

_____

_____

I will Take Action by:

_____

_____

_____

My study will begin on _____.

Date

My goal is to finish by _____.

Date

_____   _____
Student Signature   Teacher Signature

TARGET ACTIVITY

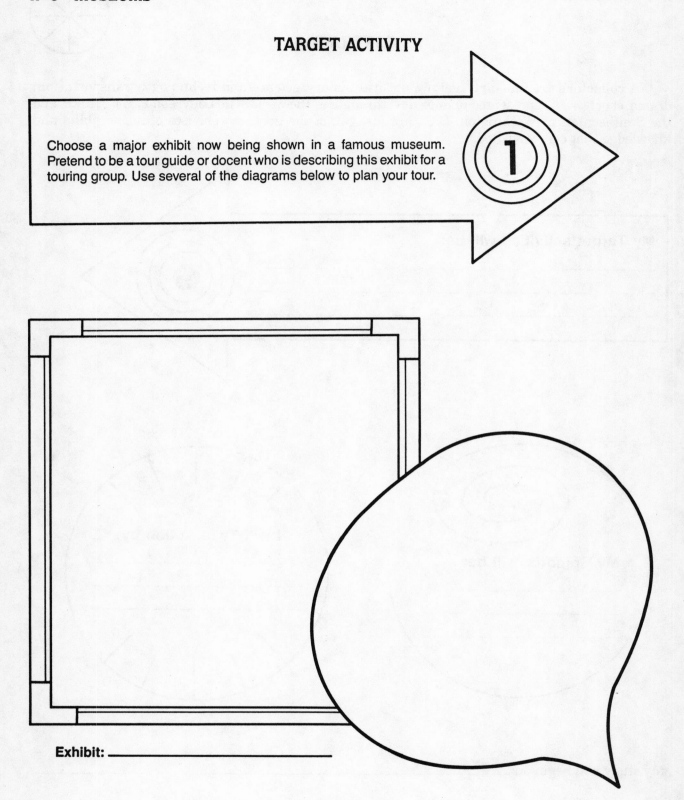

Choose a major exhibit now being shown in a famous museum. Pretend to be a tour guide or docent who is describing this exhibit for a touring group. Use several of the diagrams below to plan your tour.

Exhibit: _____

To be more creative, try being the exhibit itself, and give the touring group information from that point of view.

TARGET ACTIVITY

Choose five different types of famous museums to study. Gather information and design pamphlets for each. Follow the form below for each selected museum.

MUSEUM NAME:

LOCATION:

ORIGIN:

COLLECTIONS THAT CAN BE VIEWED:

OTHER INTERESTING FACTS ABOUT THIS MUSEUM:

Share the pamphlets with the class and/or send each of them to the appropriate museum studied.

TARGET ACTIVITY

What types of jobs are available in a museum? What qualifications are necessary? Research to find out, and create advertisements for three different positions.

Position 1:

Position 2:

Position 3:

TARGET ACTIVITY

Philanthropists are people who donate large sums of money for charitable purposes. Study about someone who established a famous museum; then be that person in a dramatization. Tell why you chose to use your money for this purpose.

Design a special philanthropic "certificate of merit"!

SPINOFF SELECTIONS

Select one of these topics for further research about museums.

Henry Ward	taxidermy	Smithsonian Institute Museums
George Peabody	King Tut Exhibit	National Baseball Hall of Fame and Museum
Gertrude V. Whitney	Mona Lisa	Metropolitan Museum of Art
Solomon Guggenheim	Art Gallery of Ontario	American Museum of Natural History
Marshall Field I	British Museum	Williamsburg, Virginia
philanthrophist	The Prado	St. Augustine, Florida
curator	The Louvre	Biltmore House, Asheville, North Carolina
docent	National Gallery of Art	Royal Canadian Academy of Arts

Use this space to record your information.

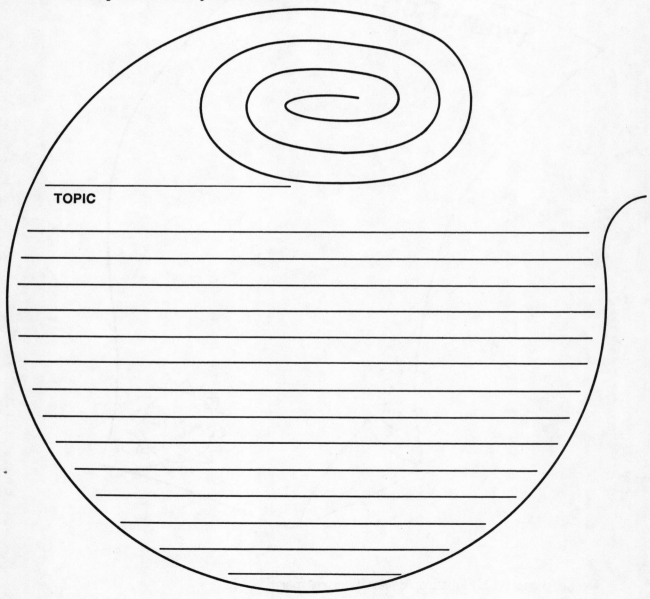

TOPIC

©1988 by The Center for Applied Research in Education

TAKE ACTION

Survey people of all ages. Ask them why they visit museums and what types of exhibits they enjoy most. Compile your information and share the results with your local museum(s). The museum staff may find it helpful for future planning and advertising purposes!

OR

If there are no museums in your area, send the survey to the mayor; perhaps it will help start one!

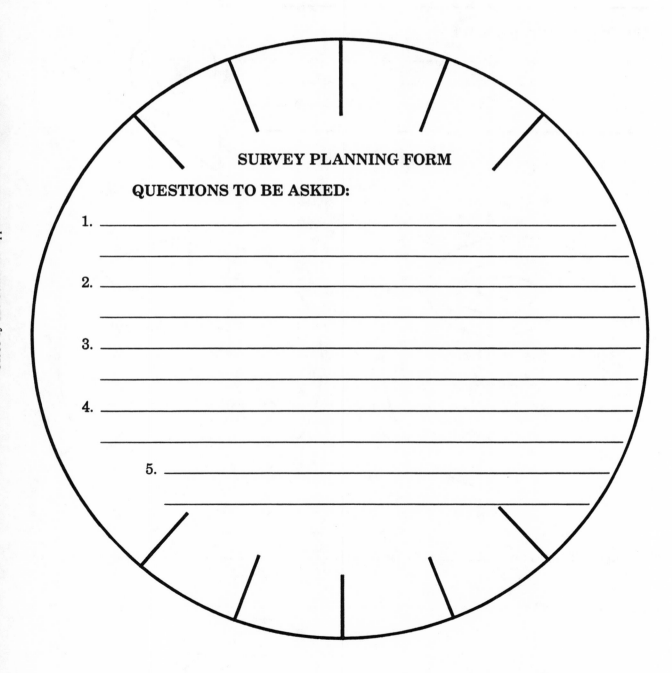

SURVEY PLANNING FORM

QUESTIONS TO BE ASKED:

1. _____

    _____

2. _____

    _____

3. _____

    _____

4. _____

    _____

    5. _____

CONTRACT

Since ancient times, the rivers of the world have been a major force in determining the shape of the earth's land and in influencing the progress of civilizations. Rivers have served as highways, a source of irrigation, food, and energy, and have long had religious importance for many people. From "shooting the rapids" to generating electricity, our life styles today are still influenced by the rivers of the world.

My Target activities will be:

_____
_____
_____

My Spinoffs will be:

_____
_____
_____

I will Take Action by:

_____
_____
_____

My study will begin on _____.
Date

My goal is to finish by _____.
Date

_____   _____
Student Signature   Teacher Signature

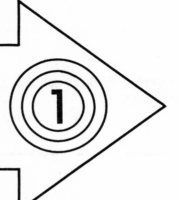

TARGET ACTIVITY

Throughout history, it has been a challenge for people to "tame" a river. Bridges, dams, dikes, and altering the channel are some of the methods used. Read about one of these attempts and describe it from the river's point of view.

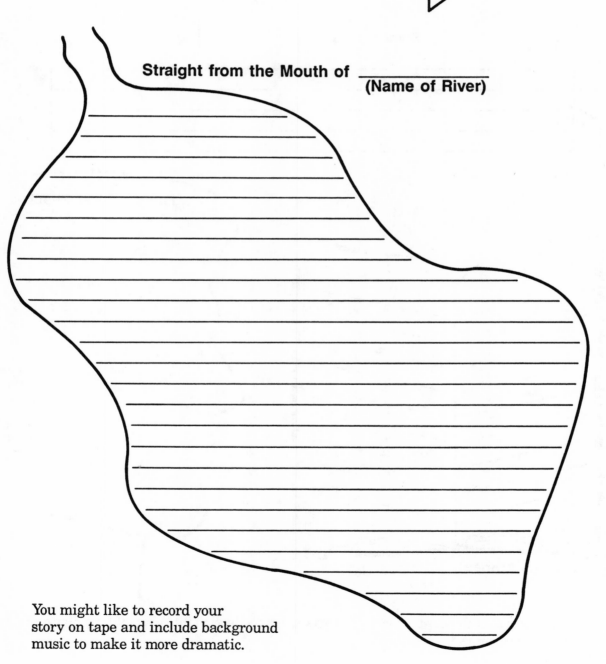

Straight from the Mouth of _____
(Name of River)

You might like to record your
story on tape and include background
music to make it more dramatic.

TARGET ACTIVITY

Make a collection of songs, stories, and people associated with life on or near rivers.

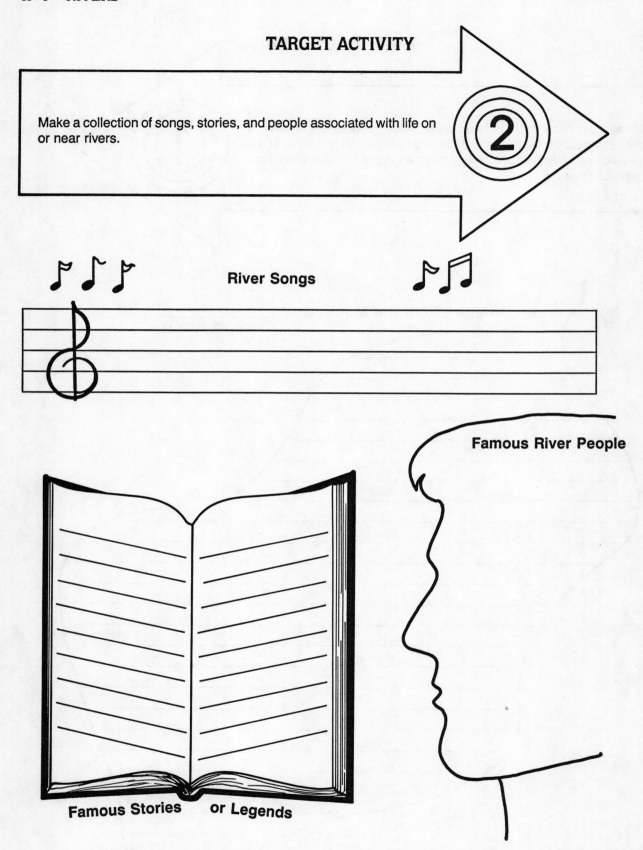

River Songs

Famous River People

Famous Stories   or Legends

Combine several of the most interesting parts of your collection into a script for a play or movie. Share this as a class project.

TARGET ACTIVITY

Research a major river system of the world and make a multimedia presentation (maps, pictures, models, and the like) that shows the river's effects on people and the land.

Forms of Transportation

Recreation and Scenic Areas

Agricultural Uses

Industrial Uses

Ports or Structures

Facts and Figures

Disasters

**SCHOOL OF EDUCATION
CURRICULUM LABORATORY
UM-DEARBORN**

TARGET ACTIVITY

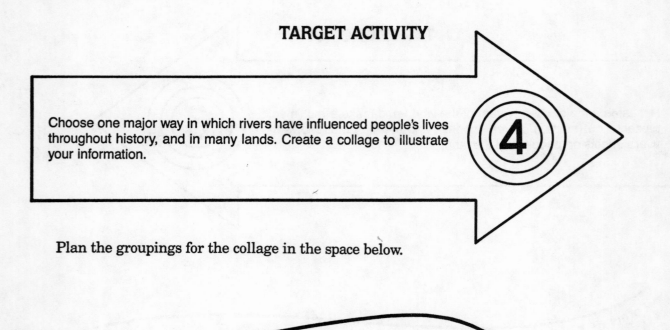

Choose one major way in which rivers have influenced people's lives throughout history, and in many lands. Create a collage to illustrate your information.

Plan the groupings for the collage in the space below.

Be sure to include symbols, colors, or other techniques to show the passage of time and/or different cultures.

SPINOFF SELECTIONS

Select one these topics for further research about rivers.

canyons	rapids	water power	Mark Twain
cataracts	erosion	basin	Stephen Collins Foster
waterfalls	dams	levee	Mike Fink
bayous	reservoirs	delta	Tennessee Valley
bridges	floods	U.S. Corps of	Authority
irrigation	national parks	Engineers	Welland Ship Canal
St. Lawrence Seaway			

Use this space to record your information.

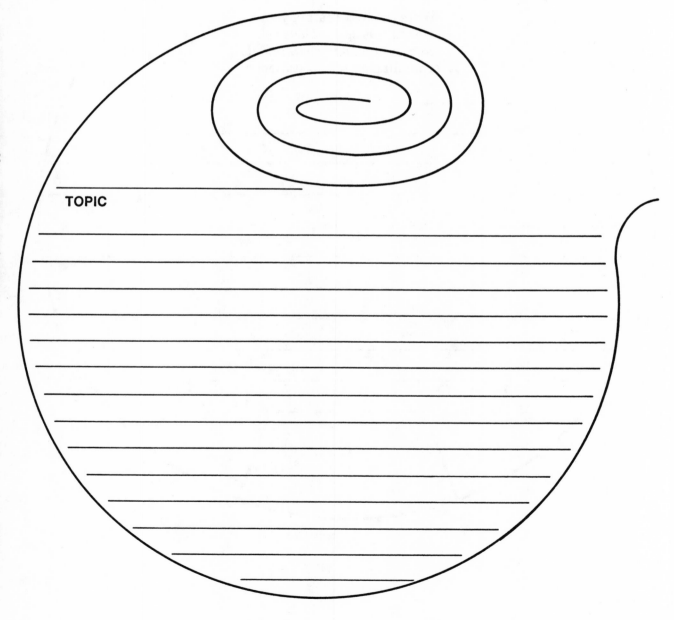

TOPIC

TAKE ACTION

Pollution is the number one enemy of our world's rivers. Research methods being used in your state to control or clean up pollution. Then write to your state representatives and express your concern for legislation in this area. (Legislators' addresses can be found in the information pages of the phone book, or by calling the local library.)

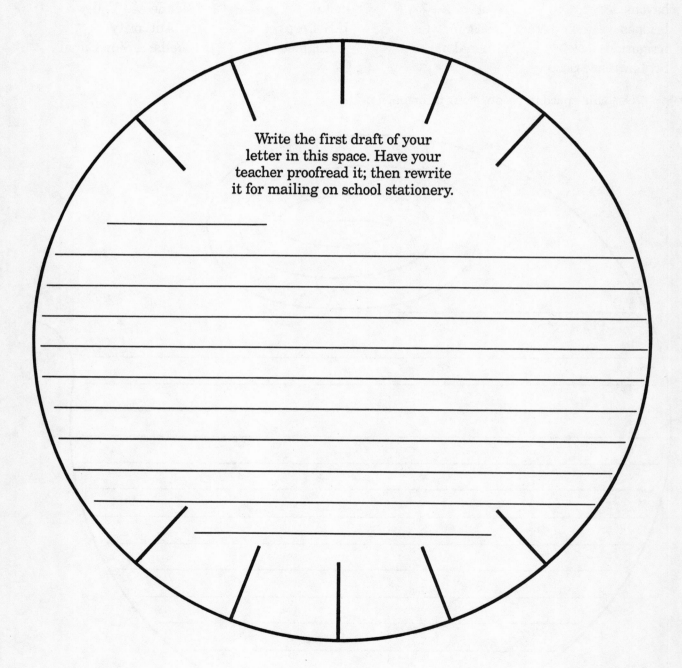

Write the first draft of your letter in this space. Have your teacher proofread it; then rewrite it for mailing on school stationery.

CONTRACT

"Oh wondrous sights—standing through the ages! How have you survived these long periods of time? What was your purpose?" Such are the thoughts one has when viewing ancient wonders; remnants of cultures long since passed. They spark the imagination and overwhelm us with their grandeur.

My Target activities will be:

_____
_____
_____

My Spinoffs will be:

_____
_____
_____

I will Take Action by:

_____
_____
_____

My study will begin on _____.
                                    Date

My goal is to finish by _____.
                                    Date

_____   _____
Student Signature   Teacher Signature

TARGET ACTIVITY

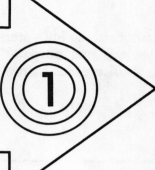

There are 7 recognized wonders of the ancient world. Research each of these to identify the location, original purpose for construction, and historical significance. Which is your favorite? Rank them from 1-7.

Make seven copies of the following form.

ANCIENT WONDER #_____

LOCATION:

ORIGINAL PURPOSE FOR CONSTRUCTION:

HISTORICAL SIGNIFICANCE:

TARGET ACTIVITY

Look for similarities and differences in these 7 ancient wonders. What factors, in your opinion, cause something to be considered a "wonder of the world"? Write an essay about "wonders" which includes both fact and opinion.

WONDER	SIMILARITIES	DIFFERENCES

TARGET ACTIVITY

Pretend that the United Nations is sponsoring a contest to select an 8th ancient wonder, to promote awareness and preservation of international wonders. As a contest committee member, how would the following questions be answered?

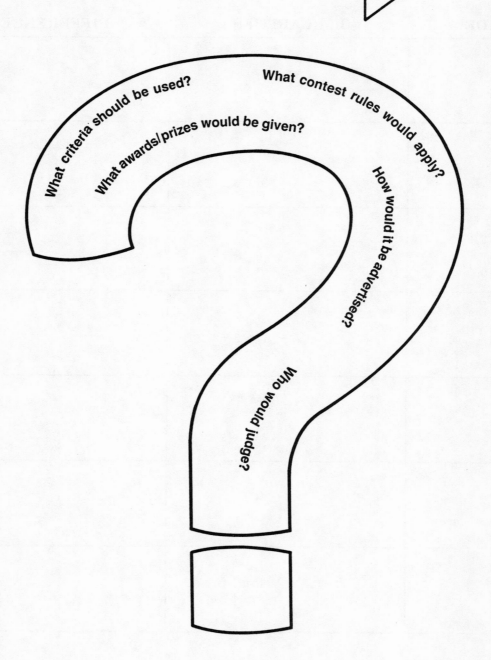

What criteria should be used?

What contest rules would apply?

What awards/prizes would be given?

How would it be advertised?

Who would judge?

TARGET ACTIVITY

Compile a list of 7 Wonderful Historic Events. Support each entry with facts about its impact on the well-being of the peoples of the Earth.

_____

is designated a WONDERFUL HISTORIC EVENT because

_____

_____

_____

_____

_____

_____

Proclaimed this day of_____

By_____

SPINOFF SELECTIONS

Select one of these topics for further research about wonders of the world.

ancient civilizations	Mayan and Aztec Pyramids	Stonehenge
Atlantis	Machu Picchu	Coliseum
Parthenon	Great Wall of China	7 Natural Wonders
Stones of Easter Island	7 Modern Wonders	Niagara Falls

Use this space to record your information.

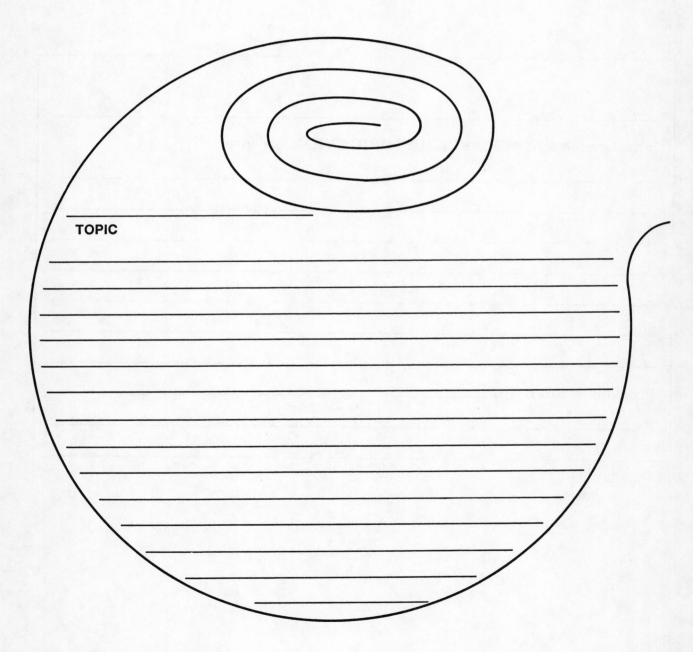

TOPIC

TAKE ACTION

Imagine yourself 75 years into the future. You are in charge of selecting 7 modern wonders of this future world. What will they be? Gather classmates' opinions about what they think 7 wonders would be.

Compare their predictions with yours and make a presentation about the 7 most popular choices. Use the space below to list your 7 predictions.

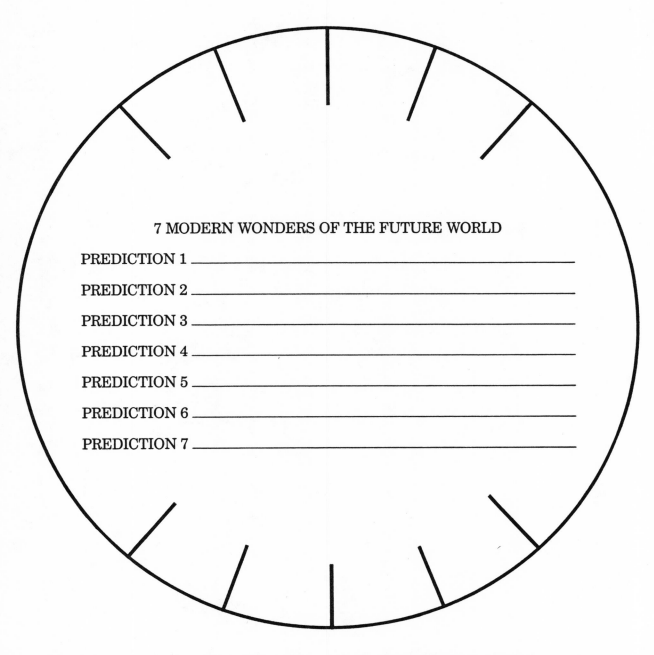

7 MODERN WONDERS OF THE FUTURE WORLD

PREDICTION 1 _____

PREDICTION 2 _____

PREDICTION 3 _____

PREDICTION 4 _____

PREDICTION 5 _____

PREDICTION 6 _____

PREDICTION 7 _____

Wish everyone a long life so all of you can be around to check on your predictions!

Number Magic

MATH PROJECTS

III–1   Architecture
III–2   Bridges
III–3   Camping
III–4   Making Games

III–5   Math-E-Magic
III–6   Optical Illusions
III–7   The Stock Market

CONTRACT

Only people have the capacity to create. The architect translates his or her creativity and uses problem solving for the designs he or she plans in homes, office buildings, churches, and factories we see around us. The architect must meet the challenge of designing buildings that are well-planned for use and safety, as well as pleasing to the eye of the client. Mathematics is part of the "language" used by architects to communicate their ideas!

My Target activities will be:

_____

_____

_____

My Spinoffs will be:

_____

_____

_____

I will Take Action by:

_____

_____

_____

My study will begin on _____.

Date

My goal is to finish by _____.

Date

_____   _____
Student Signature   Teacher Signature

TARGET ACTIVITY

Research the training and educational requirements necessary to become an architect and make a note file of information. Include pictures of the special "tools of the trade" used by architects. Role play this occupation for classmates when you are finished!

(1)

Notes: **Education**

Notes: **Training**

Notes: **Tools**

TARGET ACTIVITY

Geometry is closely related to architectural form. Create the "ideal home" using geometric shapes for the design. Draw a blueprint of your plan using a scale of 1/4 inch = 1 foot. Consider special features and rooms the home will have. Label these in the plan.

PLAN FOR AN IDEAL HOME

Show your plan to someone in the construction business. Ask them what they think of it.

TARGET ACTIVITY

The "Golden Section"* was an important geometric feature of ancient Greek architecture. It was used in repeated designs for the structure of temples, columns, and decorative sculpture. Our understanding of ratio and proportion comes from this early use. Write a brief report explaining the "Golden Section." Draw examples of its use.

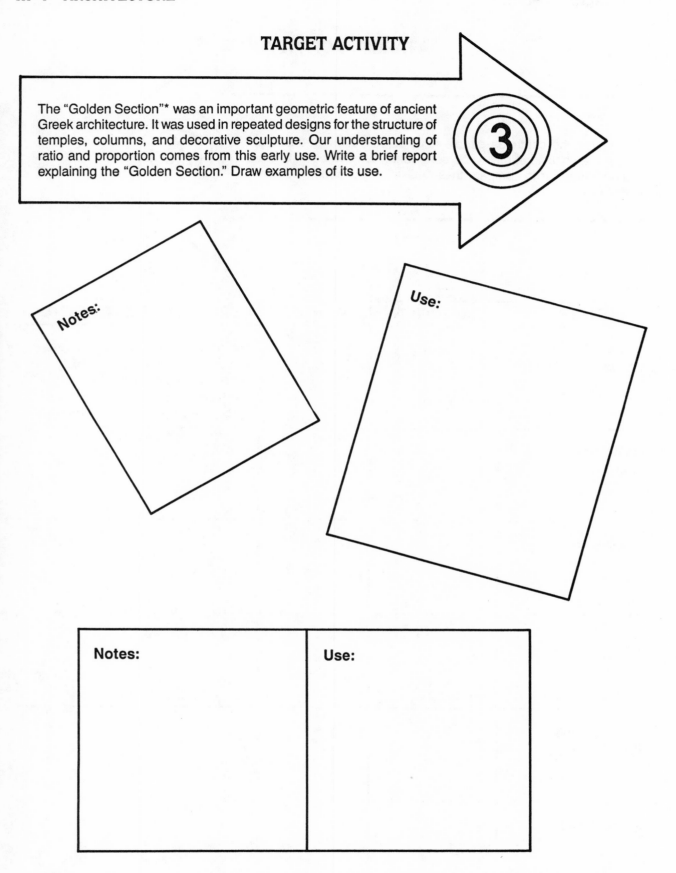

Notes:

Use:

Notes:	Use:

*The "Golden Section" is also referred to as the Golden Ratio or the Golden Proportion.

TARGET ACTIVITY

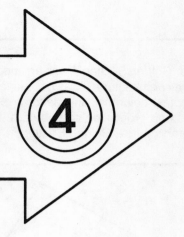

Throughout the centuries people have created many monumental works of architecture, still to be seen today. Do some reading and research in order to compare these massive structures. (See completed example.)

STRUCTURE	LOCATION	HEIGHT	STRUCTURAL STATISTICS
Pyramid of Cheops	Cairo, Egypt	160′	has an area of 10 football fields weighs about 5 million tons there are approximately 2½ million stones took about 30 years to build
The Porcelain Pagoda			
Hagia Sophia			
Empire State Building			
United Nations Building			
Imperial Hotel			

SPINOFF SELECTIONS

Select one of these topics for further research about Architecture.

Michelangelo	R. Buckminster Fuller	Arch
Thomas Jefferson	Frank Lloyd Wright	Column
Richard M. Hunt	I. M. Pei	Dome
John Root	Philip Johnson	Cantilever
Louis Sullivan	James Stirling	Vault
Walter Gropius	Pier Luigi Nervi	Kenzo Tange

Use this space to record your information.

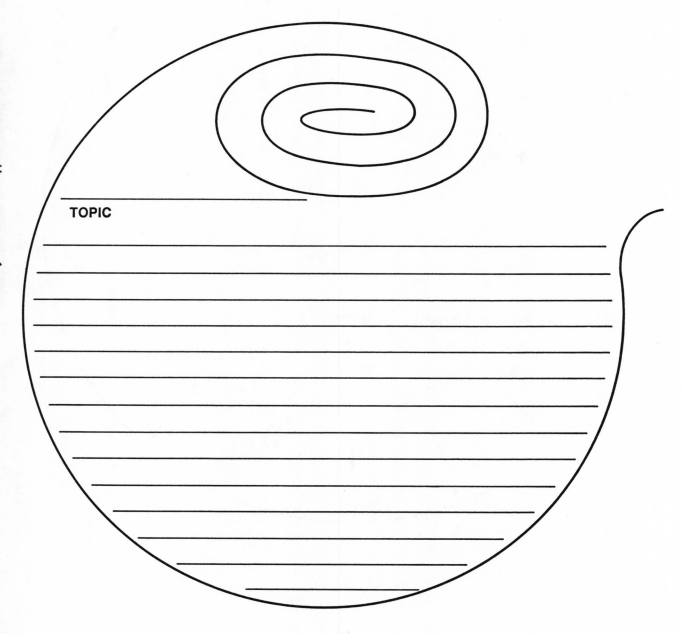

TOPIC

TAKE ACTION

Set up an architectural center in the classroom. Include books, filmstrips, models of shapes, puzzles, pictures, and work you have done in the Target activities. What else could be added to make the center more interesting? Organize your ideas below.

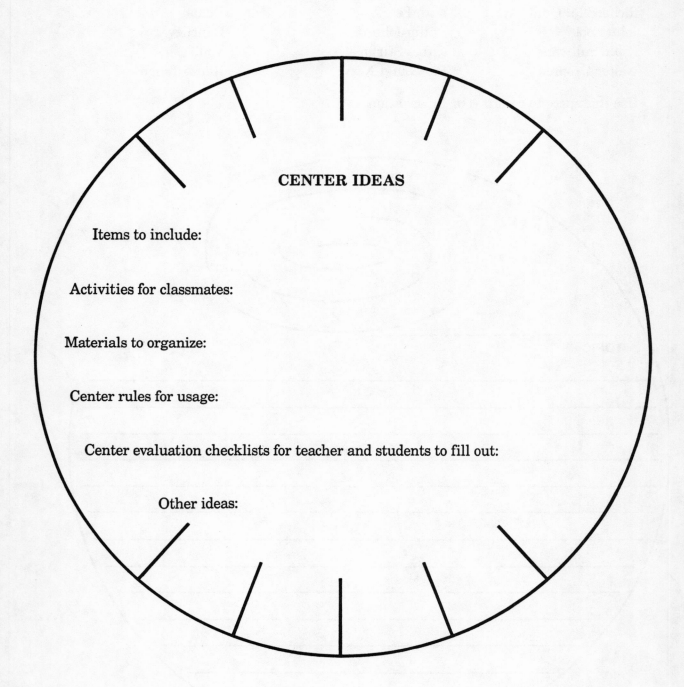

CENTER IDEAS

Items to include:

Activities for classmates:

Materials to organize:

Center rules for usage:

Center evaluation checklists for teacher and students to fill out:

Other ideas:

CONTRACT

The term "bridge" has many meanings. It can be a card game, a structure used by people to cross a body of water, a connection or transition from one time to another, or a raised platform on a boat. Many of us use bridges daily in our travel to and from our work or our homes. Some of these engineering marvels such as the Brooklyn Bridge or the Golden Gate Bridge have inspired photographers and writers for years.

My Target activities will be:

_____
_____
_____

My Spinoffs will be:

_____
_____
_____

I will Take Action by:

_____
_____
_____

My study will begin on _____
Date

My goal is to finish by _____
Date

_____   _____
Student Signature   Teacher Signature

TARGET ACTIVITY

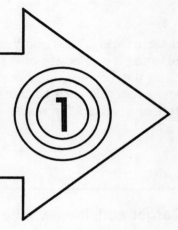

Bridges vary in structure, height, length of span, and purpose, depending on where they are built. Make a comparison chart of some well-known bridges. Select one and draw a sketch of it.

BRIDGE	LOCATION	YEAR BUILT	HEIGHT ABOVE WATER	LENGTH (SPAN)
GOLDEN GATE				
BROOKLYN				
VERRAZANO				
GEORGE WASHINGTON				
TACOMA				
MACKINAC				

WORD PROBLEMS·

TARGET ACTIVITY

Find and arrange bridge terms dealing with construction or structure as a word search for classmates to solve. Use a large grid to plan the word search. Don't forget to list words used at the side!

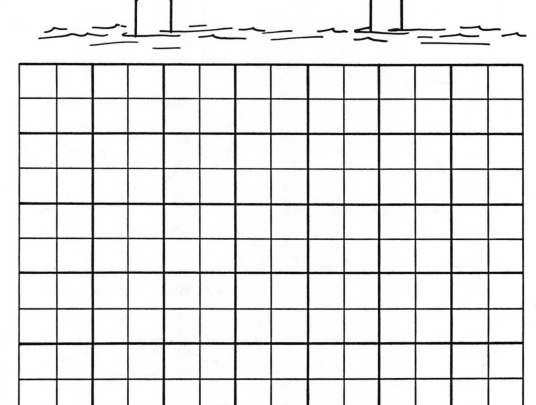

WORD LIST

_____
_____
_____
_____
_____
_____
_____
_____
_____
_____
_____
_____
_____

TARGET ACTIVITY

Construct a three-dimensional model of one type of bridge. Decide on the scale to be used in order to estimate overall size if this bridge were actually constructed! Give it a name when finished.

③

SCALE = _____   NAME _____

POSSIBLE CONSTRUCTION MATERIALS

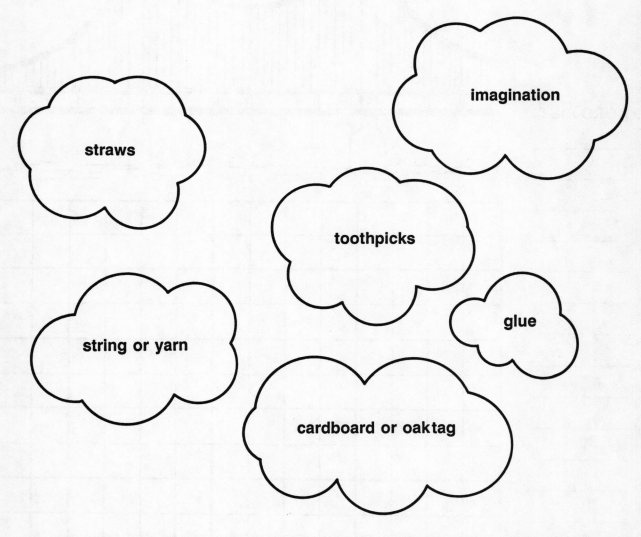

straws

imagination

toothpicks

glue

string or yarn

cardboard or oaktag

How much weight could this bridge hold? Think of a way to test the model when it is completed.

TARGET ACTIVITY

4

Compile a "Book of Records" illustrating interesting and unusual bridge facts. Topics might include: oldest bridge, longest, first of its kind, hardest to build, history, and unusual problems encountered during construction.

Display this book in your classroom to be shared with others.

SPINOFF SELECTIONS

Select one of these topics for further research about Bridges.

suspension bridge	simple beam bridge	London Bridge
arch bridge	swinging bridge	Bridge of Sighs
truss bridge	movable bridge	John Roebling
cantilever bridge	aqueduct	Joseph B. Strauss
tower bridge	Brooklyn Bridge	

Use this space to record your information.

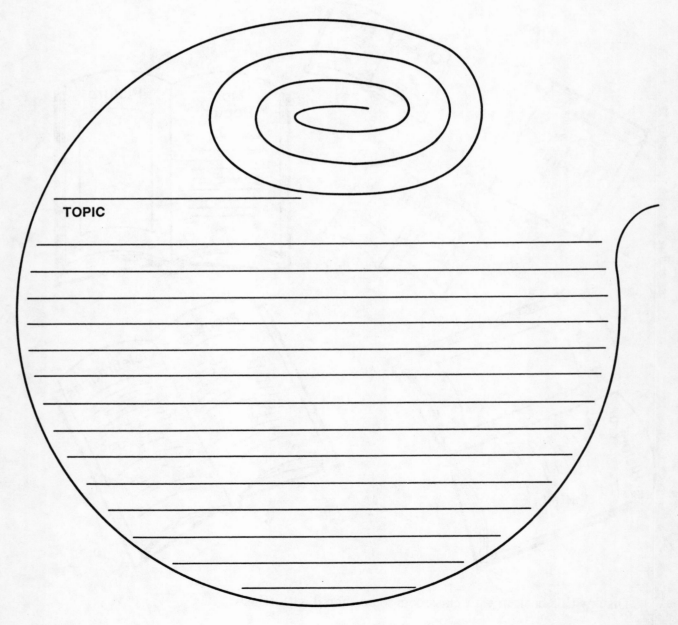

TOPIC

TAKE ACTION

Invite someone from an engineering firm as a class speaker to discuss principles of bridge design.

OR

Take a "bridge" field trip in your area. Make a few sketches of some. Try to identify the structural type of each, and the approximate height and weight.

Use the form below to plan the Take Action activity you have selected.

PLANNING STEPS

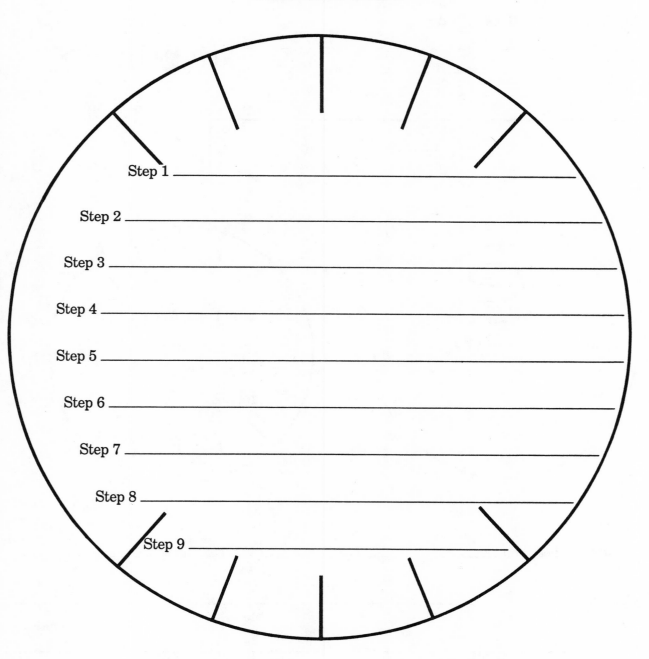

Step 1 _____

Step 2 _____

Step 3 _____

Step 4 _____

Step 5 _____

Step 6 _____

Step 7 _____

Step 8 _____

Step 9 _____

CONTRACT

The great outdoors! Communicating with "mother nature"! Camping is a wonderful family activity. It is also a great activity for kids if they go to camps during the summer.

Suppose you had all the money you needed to build a summer camp for kids, and could offer activities and camping skills necessary to make it the best camp ever. There would be many things to plan and consider. Here is a chance to design your "ideal camp."

My Target activities will be:

_____

_____

_____

My Spinoffs will be:

_____

_____

_____

I will Take Action by:

_____

_____

_____

My study will begin on _____

Date

My goal is to finish by _____

Date

_____   _____
Student Signature   Teacher Signature

TARGET ACTIVITY

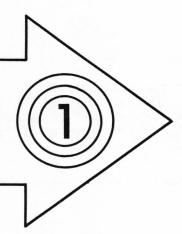

Draw a map of the camp's location. It could be a real or imaginary site. Identify major and minor cities, state boundaries, and highway routes. Include a direction compass and scale of miles. Make the map as realistic as possible! Give your camp a name.

MAP LOCATION OF CAMP_____

TARGET ACTIVITY

Pretend you are in an airplane 1000 feet above the camp. How would it appear? Draw an aerial view of what can be seen. Show any geographical features such as mountains, lakes, rivers, trails, nearby. Include cabins, dining hall, recreation areas, and any other facilities of the camp.

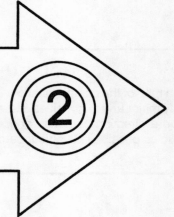

AERIAL VIEW OF CAMP

TARGET ACTIVITY

Be the "camp accountant!" In order to stay in business, profit should be made each summer! Who are the employees and what is their rate of pay per week? How many campers will be needed and at what rates in order to make a profit? Use this "ledger" style sheet to compute camp costs and determine if you will be operationally sound!

LEDGER SHEET

I	EXPENSES	TOTALS
_____ counsellors @ _____ per week each =		_____
_____ cooks/kitchen crew @ _____ per week each =		_____
_____ maintenance/grounds @ _____ per week each =		_____
_____ special instructors @ _____ per week each =		_____
_____ electric/water/garbage @ _____ per week each =		_____
_____ food/beverages @ _____ per week for _____ campers and staff—3 meals a day =		_____
* _____ (other expenses) =		_____
	TOTAL----------	_____

*Many other expenses can be included such as insurance, equipment replacement, consumable supplies, and other employees. This will be determined by the kind of camp and activities that are offered, as well as the total number of campers you have *room* to accommodate. (Be sure the aerial view in Target 2 shows enough cabins, etc. for the numbers to be handled.)

II	INCOME	TOTALS
_____ campers @ _____ per week for _____ weeks =		_____
	PROFIT/LOSS AT END OF SEASON	_____

TARGET ACTIVITY

Develop an advertising brochure describing the camp. How much will be charged? What activities are available for campers? What special clothing and equipment are needed? Does the camp have a slogan and T-shirt symbol? Use the planning sheet for ideas before you start the brochure.

PLANNING SHEET

COST PER WEEK· COST PER TWO WEEKS: COST PER MONTH.	CAMP EMBLEM AND SLOGAN
CAMP T-SHIRT SYMBOL	DAILY TIME SCHEDULE OF EVENTS
CLOTHING AND PERSONAL NEEDS	EQUIPMENT

SPINOFF SELECTIONS

Select one of these topics for further research about camping.

sports history/activities
computer camps
arts and crafts
horses/horseback riding
woodlore
canoes/canoeing
John J. Audubon

swimming safety/water sports
dramatics/stage productions
menus/balanced diet
archery
riflery
John Muir
sailing/surfing

Use this space to record your information.

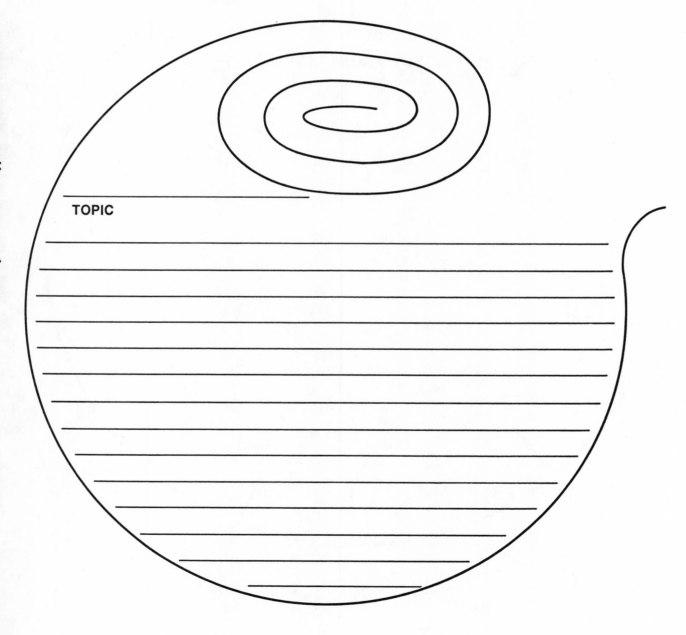

TOPIC

TAKE ACTION

Write a speech that you would give to parents convincing them to send their children to your camp. Present this speech to classmates. (Ask them to pretend that they are a group of parents!) After concluding your speech, answer any questions they may have about your camp.

Plan the major points you will make in your speech on the form below.

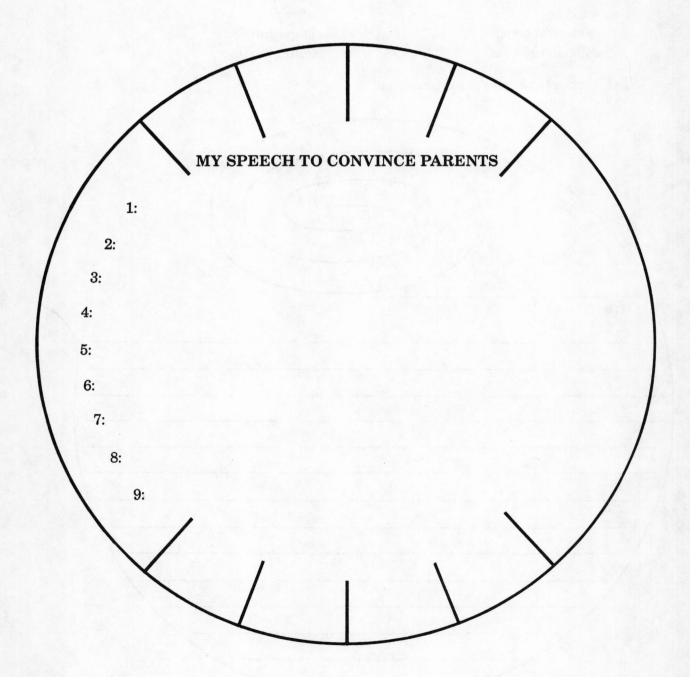

MY SPEECH TO CONVINCE PARENTS

1:

2:

3:

4:

5:

6:

7:

8:

9:

CONTRACT

Played by people for centuries, games provide us with many hours of entertainment. They enable us to sharpen thinking strategies while learning new ideas. Many games are based on mathematics through the scoring systems or playing boards used. Some are complicated to play, while others can be quite simple. Games can be used at home, in school, and wherever there are two or more people interested in playing.

My Target activities will be:

_____

_____

_____

My Spinoffs will be:

_____

_____

_____

I will Take Action by:

_____

_____

_____

My study will begin on _____.

Date

My goal is to finish by _____.

Date

_____   _____

Student Signature   Teacher Signature

TARGET ACTIVITY

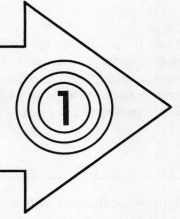

Investigate and evaluate games at school and home. Classify games according to type, scoring system, and educational value. Rank each on a 1 to 5 scale, 1 the lowest and 5 the highest. Use the chart below for this activity.

NAME OF GAME	PURPOSE	SCORING/HOW TO WIN?	EDUCATIONAL VALUE	RANKING

TARGET ACTIVITY

What's in a game? Many games are based on mathematical ideas that can be identified using a method called "webbing." (See examples.) Select any 5 sports and develop a poster display of mathematical "webs" for each. Display the completed poster in class.

(2)

TRACK EVENTS — Olympics < Records / Noted participants

Teams / Individuals

Kinds

Rate of speed

Height

Distance   Time

Throwing   Jumping

BILLIARDS — Noted players

Ball positions

Cue positions

angles   fractions

angles   fractions

? — FOOTBALL — ?

Distance

Time

Yard   Downs per Yards

Quarters

There might be other ways to do this webbing, depending on the ideas of each person. **Try to think of categories, keeping them together with a branching mark ∧ .**

TARGET ACTIVITY

Tic-Tac-Toe is a favorite paper-and-pencil game. There are many others that can offer much fun and strategy of play such as "Curvers," a game based on Topology, the mathematical study of surfaces. Get a partner, read the directions below, and start playing!

©1988 by The Center for Applied Research in Education

PLAYING DIRECTIONS FOR "CURVERS"

You may not have more than four curves coming from any dot. A curved line may not cut across any other curved line.

EXPLANATION OF PLAY	DIAGRAM

1. Draw a curved line. Enlarge the starting and ending points (A,B) and place large midpoint (C) on the curve.

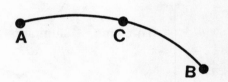

2. The first person to go draws a curved line between any 2 points (B,C) then places a new midpoint on the curve (D).

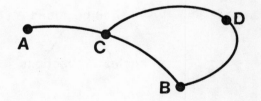

3. The next person takes a turn doing the same thing. Continue in this manner until there are no points left to use. The last person to make a move is the game winner.

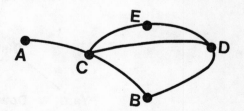

Note: Point C can no longer be used.

Can you create other variations of this game? Could more than 2 people play at a time? Could 4 points be started with instead of 3? What do you think? Experiment with "Curvers" and see what can be done.

TARGET ACTIVITY

Design and make an original game. First decide if it will be a board game or card game. Provide clear instructions for players, scoring, cards, and pieces necessary. The game should have a mathematical basis—possibly related to a current topic being studied in mathematics. Will this be a board game? card game? Decide first!

Board Game?

Card Game?

Game Name _____

Object of game/Scoring/Size of board:

Instructions:

Playing pieces needed and size:

Extra cards and equipment:

Decorations/Illustration ideas:

    Try the finished game with classmates. Did they understand the rules of play? Did they enjoy playing?

SPINOFF SELECTIONS

Select one of these topics for further research about games.

card games	learning games	early Colonial games
board games	puzzles	brainteasers
billiards	paper and pencil games	games of other countries
TV game shows	current popular games	games from ancient times

Use this space to record your information.

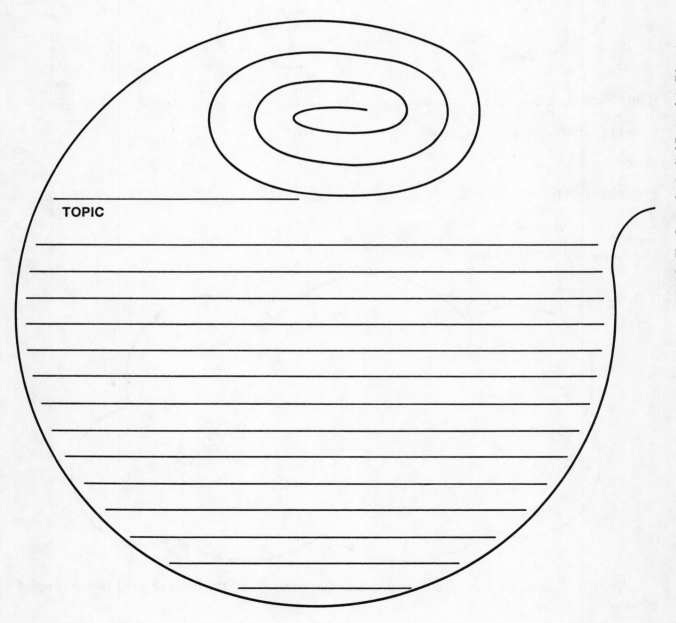

TOPIC

TAKE ACTION

Bring your original game to a local toy store and show it to the manager. Ask for suggestions and comments. Find out how you might improve the game. Record the suggestions and comments on the form below.

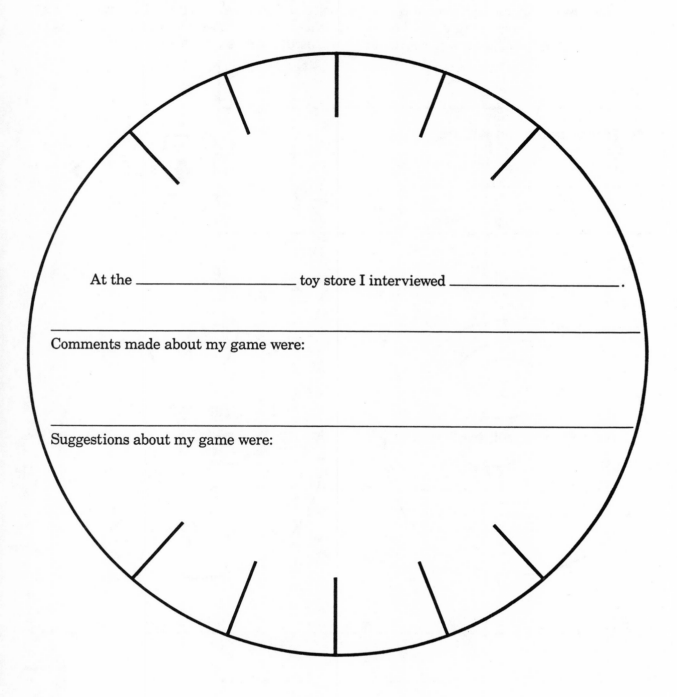

At the _____ toy store I interviewed _____.

Comments made about my game were:

Suggestions about my game were:

CONTRACT

Galileo once stated, "Mathematics is the language with which man has written the universe!" This universal language helps us create order from chaos. It conforms to set rules and procedures. It is a precise way of expression, from the telling of time to the calculations of vast distances beyond our galaxy.

Many interesting and unusual processes and patterns have been discovered about numbers by mathematicians who lived long ago. They experimented and searched for unusual patterns and arrangements that are astonishing even today as we discover and study them!

My Target activities will be:
_____
_____
_____

My Spinoffs will be:
_____
_____
_____

I will Take Action by:
_____
_____
_____

My study will begin on _____.
　　　　　　　　　　　　　　　　Date

My goal is to finish by _____.
　　　　　　　　　　　　　　　　Date

_____　　　　　_____
Student Signature　　　　　　　　　　Teacher Signature

TARGET ACTIVITY

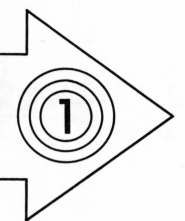

The body of mathematics knowledge was developed by ancient Greeks, the "senior citizens" of mathematics! The rules and procedures are universal, enabling us to communicate our ideas. Select any two from the list to write a "mini-biography" about, and set up a demonstration showing a major contribution of each.

SENIOR CITIZENS OF MATHEMATICS

Thales Of Miletus   Euclid   Pythagoras
Erastothenes   Plato

_____

"MINI-BIO" NOTES:

DEMONSTRATIONS WILL INCLUDE:

TARGET ACTIVITY

Tautonyms are patterned products found when multiplying with ones and zeros such as 101 × 59 = 5959! Discover others below, then try creating and experimenting with new tautonyms of your own. (There are also tautonym words—murmur, bonbon, mama—can you add to the list?)

TAUTONYM PROBLEMS	WORK SPACE	ANSWERS
101 × 34 =		
1001 × 135 =		
10101 × 61 =		
10101 × 83 =		
101 × 78 =		

What do you notice about the relationship between the tautonym problem and the answers?

TAUTONYMS OF MY OWN

TAUTONYM WORDS

©1988 by The Center for Applied Research in Education

TARGET ACTIVITY

Search mathematics books for unusual patterns. Make a set of flash cards showing the patterns you have discovered. Start with the patterns below.

Can you complete each pattern and predict the next few lines? What clues help you do this?

$8 \times 88 =$	$8 \times 888 =$	$8 \times 8888 =$	$8 \times 88888 =$	$8 \times 888888 =$	Next ?
$3 \times 37 =$	$6 \times 37 =$	$9 \times 37 =$	$12 \times 37 =$	$15 \times 37 =$	Next ?

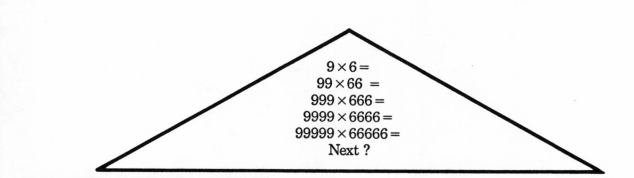

$9 \times 6 =$
$99 \times 66 =$
$999 \times 666 =$
$9999 \times 6666 =$
$99999 \times 66666 =$
Next ?

$111 \times 111 =$
$111 \times 121 =$
$111 \times 131 =$
$111 \times 141 =$
$111 \times 151 =$
Next ?

$0 \times 9 + 1 =$
$1 \times 9 + 2 =$
$12 \times 9 + 3 =$
$123 \times 9 + 4 =$
$1234 \times 9 + 5 =$
$12345 \times 9 + 6 =$
Next?

TARGET ACTIVITY

Develop a new number system. Name it after yourself. Create a special symbol for 0, 5, 10, 100, and 1000.

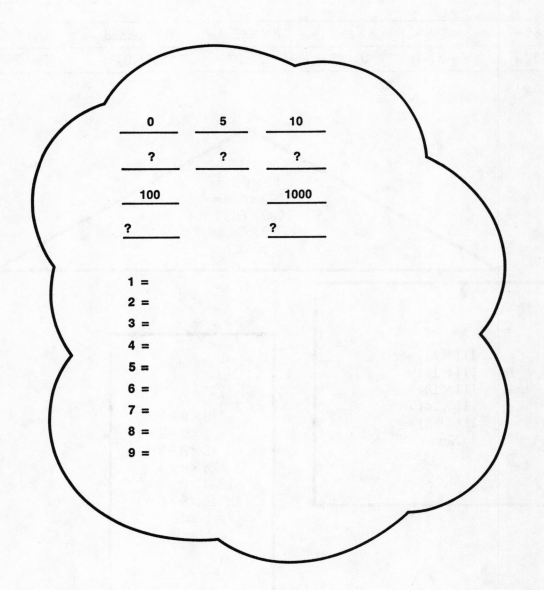

0	5	10
?	?	?

100	1000
?	?

1 =

2 =

3 =

4 =

5 =

6 =

7 =

8 =

9 =

Write some number problems using the new "_____" system.

SPINOFF SELECTIONS

Select one of these topics for further research about mathematics.

Goldbach's Conjecture	Fibonacci Sequence
Napier's Rods	Tanagrams
Pascal's Triangle	Magic Squares
Moscow Papyrus	Topology
Rhind Papyrus	Symmetry
Tesselations/Escher	Blaise Pascal
René Descartes	Albert Einstein

Use this space to record your information.

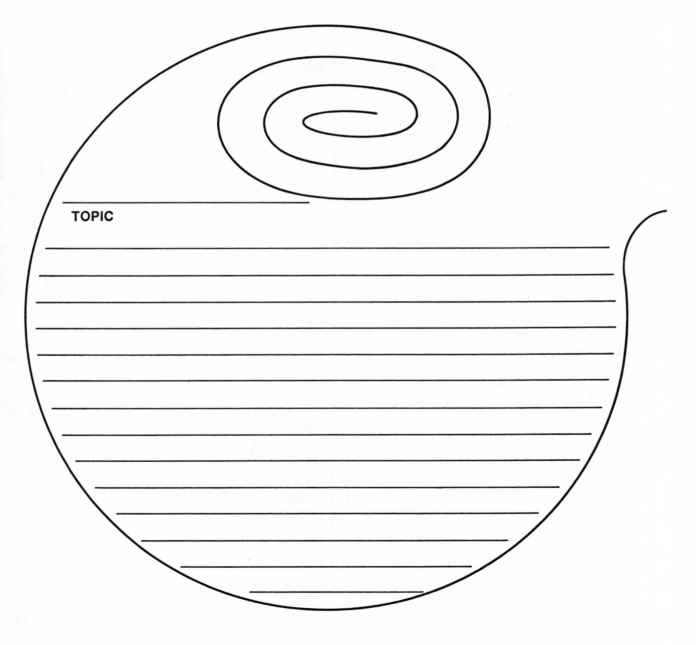

TOPIC

TAKE ACTION

Teach a number pattern lesson to your class! First get permission from the teacher and set up a date and time to do this. Develop a lesson plan from the activities you completed. Make flash cards, charts, transparencies, or other visual aids to make this lesson interesting.

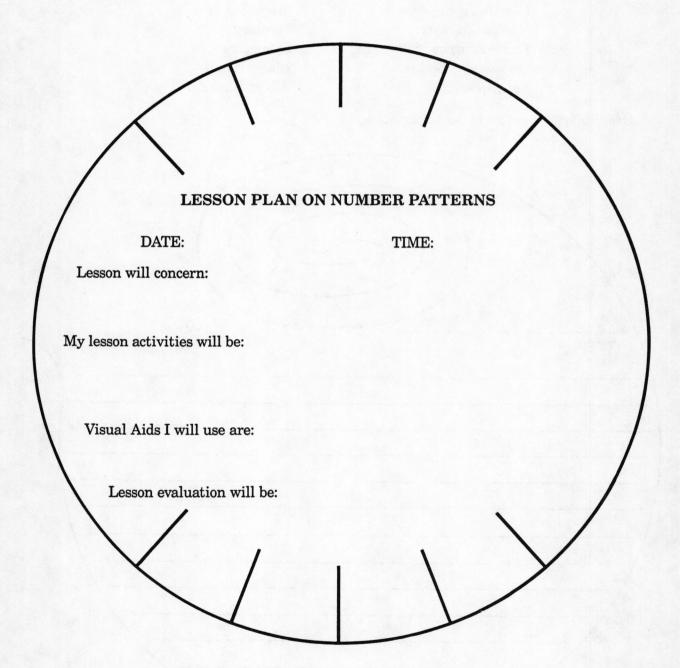

LESSON PLAN ON NUMBER PATTERNS

DATE: TIME:

Lesson will concern:

My lesson activities will be:

Visual Aids I will use are:

Lesson evaluation will be:

CONTRACT

Do your eyes play tricks on you? Can you see what is not really there?

Optical illusions cause this to happen. Color, size, and length of lines of objects affect what your eyes see. Illusions are strange, baffling, tricky, and amazing. Trying to draw an illusion can be as difficult a task as looking at one—depending on your perception of depth and your ability to measure accurately.

My Target activities will be:

_____

_____

_____

My Spinoffs will be:

_____

_____

_____

I will Take Action by:

_____

_____

_____

My study will begin on _____.

Date

My goal is to finish by _____.

Date

_____   _____

Student Signature   Teacher Signature

TARGET ACTIVITY

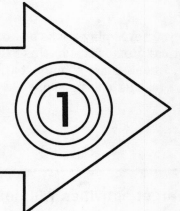

Accurate measurement is one important method used when determining illusions. Observe the illusions below and use a ruler to help answer the questions.

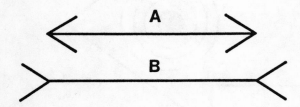

Which arrow line is longer? _____

What causes this illusion? _____

Is line (a) longer or shorter than line (b) ?

What is the exact measurement of each?

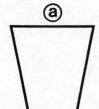

(a)

(b)

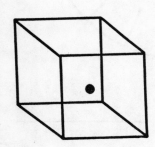

The solid circle might seem to be in the lower back right corner. Or is it in the center of the front side? How can you tell? Try to describe the *position* of each using measurement terms.

_____

_____

_____

_____

TARGET ACTIVITY

Make a picture collection of optical illusions that you find in books.
Describe the factors causing each to be an illusion.

Illusion:	Illusion:
Cause:	Cause:
Illusion:	Illusion:
Cause:	Cause:
Illusion:	Illusion:
Cause:	Cause:

Find out how the human eye works. What is it in the eye that helps us see illusions?

TARGET ACTIVITY

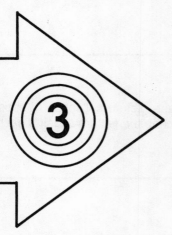

Draw an illusion of your own after you have studied several illusions. Plan it out on art paper. Be sure to use a ruler to measure and draw all parts of it.

My Original Illusion

Experiment with different colors in your original illusion. Are there any colors that affect the illusion more than others?

TARGET ACTIVITY

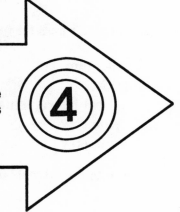

How are illusions used in magic? theater? movies? Read about these topics and record the information on note cards. Give some examples of illusions in each category.

NOTES

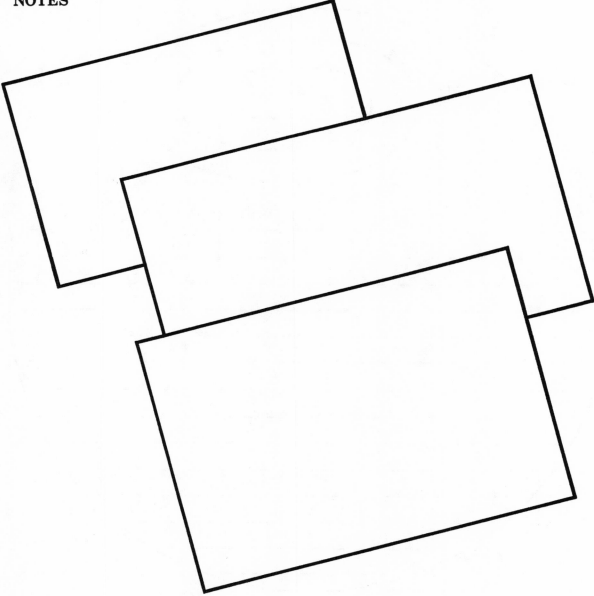

SPINOFF SELECTIONS

Select one of these topics for further research about optical illusions.

holograms	visual perception	Escher
optics	thaumatrope	Mondrian
optical instruments	stroboscope	Klee
optometry	lenses	Cubism
symmetry	tesselations	

Use this space to record your information.

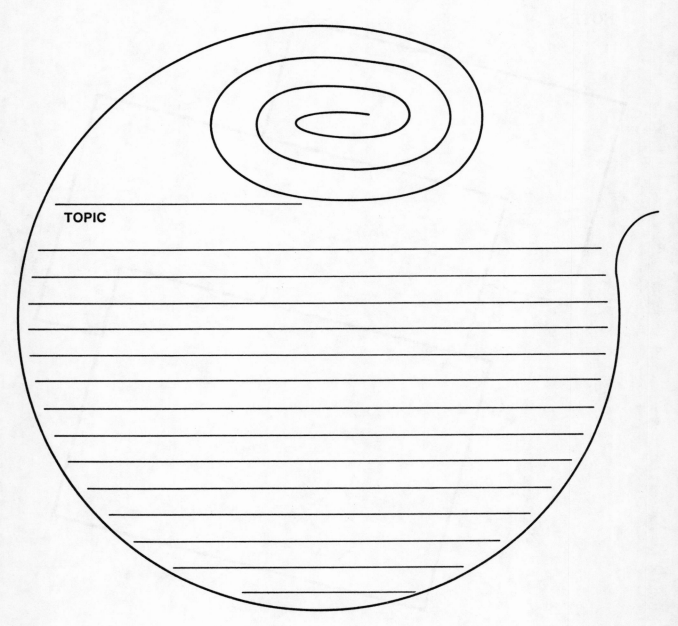

TOPIC

TAKE ACTION

Draw an enlargement on oaktag or cardboard of any illusion from the Target activities. When completed, cut it apart into jigsaw-type puzzle pieces. Put it into a decorated box for use in the classroom.

OR

Start a new fad. Draw the illusion on an old T-shirt and wear it to school (if it is appropriate to the dress code).

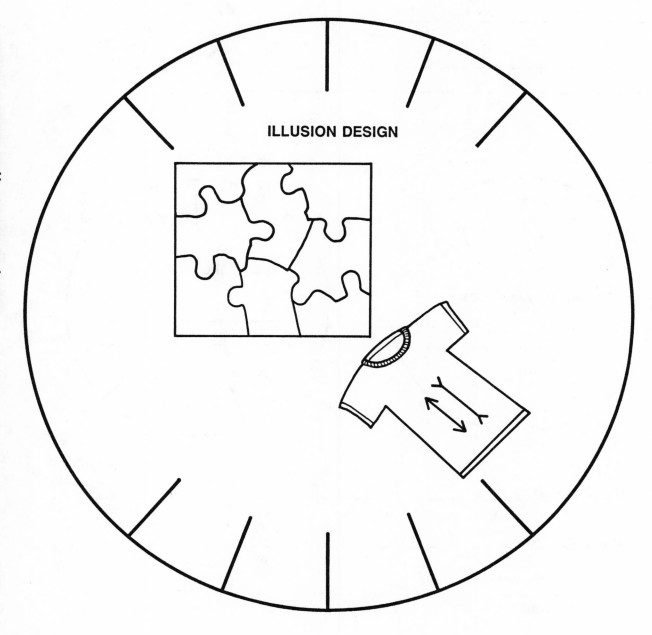

ILLUSION DESIGN

CONTRACT

Stock Exchanges play important roles in the economic life of all major industrial nations. They provide a convenient way for people to invest money by buying stock, thereby owning a share of big business. The businesses in turn use the money invested to expand and produce more goods. There are hundreds of companies to consider before you decide which stock to buy. You may make money if the company has good earnings. You may lose money if conditions are bad and the company doesn't do as well. That's the chance taken when investments are made in the Stock Market.

My Target activities will be:

_____

_____

_____

My Spinoffs will be:

_____

_____

_____

I will Take Action by:

_____

_____

_____

My study will begin on _____.

Date

My goal is to finish by _____.

Date

_____   _____
Student Signature   Teacher Signature

TARGET ACTIVITY

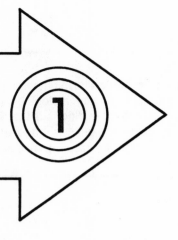

Do some reading about the Stock Exchange. Make an information sheet about its history and development from 1792 through today.

STOCK EXCHANGE INFORMATION SHEET	
YEAR	**EVENT**
1792	
Today	

Do the Take Action activity before going further. It will help you with the rest of this study.

TARGET ACTIVITY

Many stock market terms have mathematical meanings and serve as a "language" by which a stock broker can communicate the wishes of clients. Give the definitions of the terms below. (If there is a brokerage firm in your area, call and request an interview with a broker. Part of the interview might include the meanings of the terms.)

TERM	MATHEMATICAL MEANING FOR BROKERS
BEAR MARKET =	
BLUE CHIP =	
BULL MARKET =	
COMMISSIONS =	
DIVIDENDS =	
ODD LOT =	
SHARES =	
SHORT =	
STOP-ORDER =	
YIELD =	

Create an original symbol that might be used for each of the terms above. Use your imagination.

TARGET ACTIVITY

What is the "Dow Jones Average?" Watch TV news for one week and record the quotes given for the "Dow" each day. At the end of the week set up a graph to show how the market ended up for the time you watched.

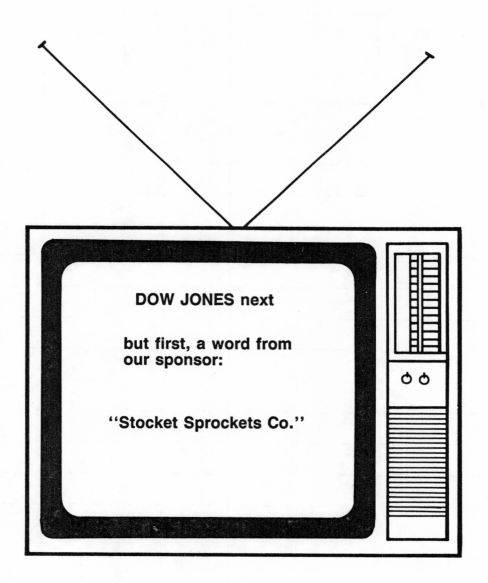

DOW JONES next

but first, a word from our sponsor:

''Stocket Sprockets Co.''

TARGET ACTIVITY

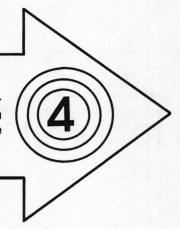

Each day newspapers list stock quotations and mathematical information about each. Select a stock and pretend you own it. Look it up each day for two weeks, recording information about it on the chart. At the end of two weeks, analyze the chart. Have you gained or lost?

DATE	FULL NAME OF STOCK	ABBREVIATION	CLOSING QUOTE	+ OR −
GAINS:			LOSSES:	

SPINOFF SELECTIONS

Select one of these topics for further research about optical illusions.

barter system
development of money
foreign currency
banking
bull/bear markets
Toronto Stock Exchange

industrial revolution
great depression
Herbert Hoover
F. D. Roosevelt
Roaring '20s

market orders
arbritration boards
American Exchange
New York Exchange
commission brokers

Use this space to record your information.

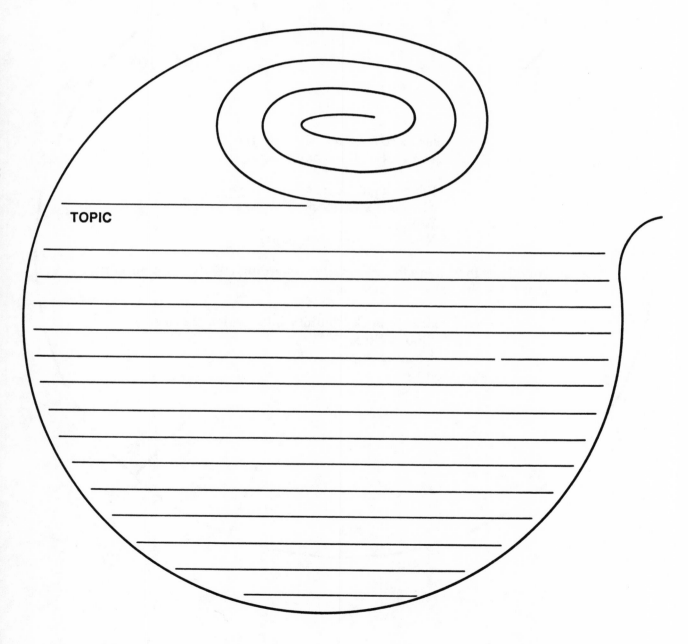

TOPIC

TAKE ACTION

You can receive a complete packet of educational materials about the New York Stock Exchange if you are interested in doing other studies about the "market." Be sure to use a business letter form, and have your teacher sign the letter too. The address is below.

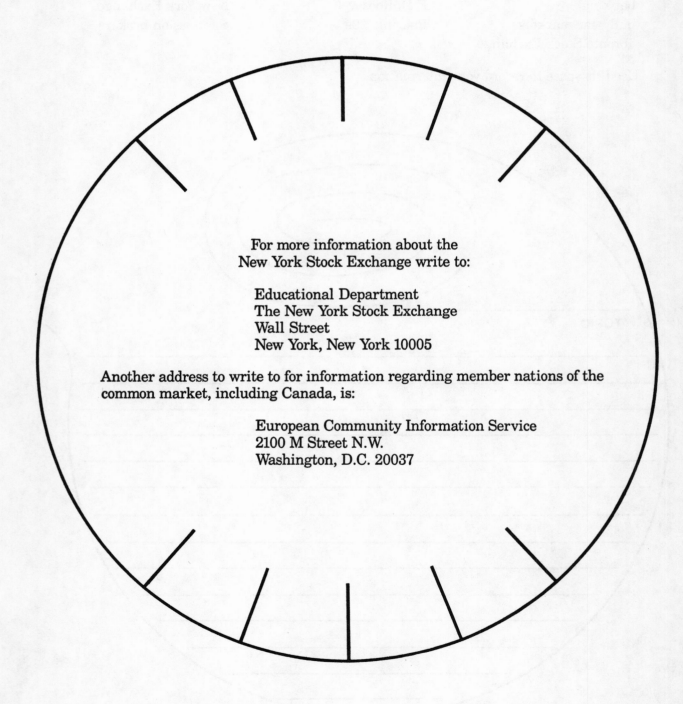

For more information about the
New York Stock Exchange write to:

Educational Department
The New York Stock Exchange
Wall Street
New York, New York 10005

Another address to write to for information regarding member nations of the common market, including Canada, is:

European Community Information Service
2100 M Street N.W.
Washington, D.C. 20037

A World of Words

LANGUAGE ARTS PROJECTS

IV–1   Advertising
IV–2   Mythology
IV–3   -Ologies
IV–4   -Onics
IV–5   Palindromes
IV–6   Phobias
IV–7   Rainbows

CONTRACT

Whether we're driving down the street, watching television, or reading a magazine, it seems that advertised messages are everywhere. These carefully designed ads inform us and try to create a need for a product or process. Through appeals to our senses and emotions, and the use of figures of speech and propaganda techniques, we, the consumers, have a hard time separating needs from persuasion.

My Target activities will be:

_____
_____
_____

My Spinoffs will be:

_____
_____
_____

I will Take Action by:

_____
_____
_____

My study will begin on _____.
                                    Date

My goal is to finish by _____.
                                    Date

_____   _____
      Student Signature   Teacher Signature

TARGET ACTIVITY

Collect at least 15 ads about a type of product—cars, food, toys, for example. Look for ways these ads are similar and different. Use the categories below to help you analyze.

1

Major words
that are the same

Words that appeal
to the senses

Adjectives

Adverbs

Type of
background used

Comparisons

Now use these notes to create an ad of your own about a chosen product. Get your classmates' responses to your original work.

TARGET ACTIVITY

Make a collection of rhymes, jingles, and famous sayings associated with ads from the past and present. Group these according to the "word play" used.

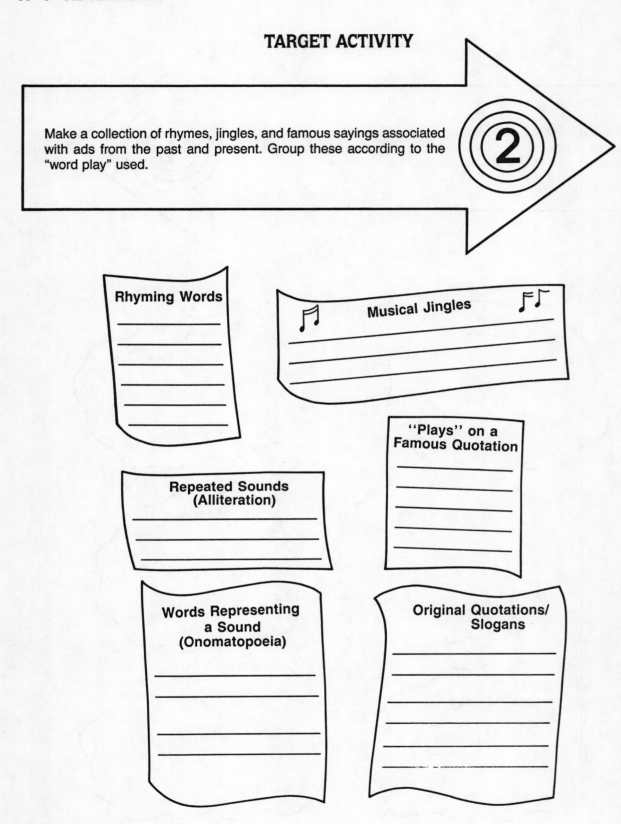

Rhyming Words

Musical Jingles

Repeated Sounds (Alliteration)

"Plays" on a Famous Quotation

Words Representing a Sound (Onomatopoeia)

Original Quotations/ Slogans

Create a game that will test your classmates' ability to associate these "word plays" with the correct product.

TARGET ACTIVITY

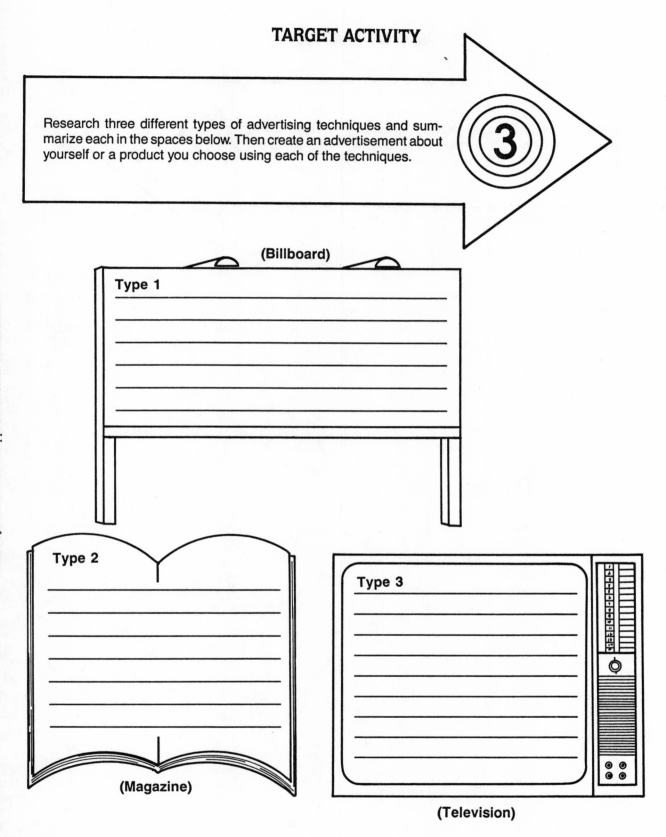

Research three different types of advertising techniques and summarize each in the spaces below. Then create an advertisement about yourself or a product you choose using each of the techniques.

③

(Billboard)

Type 1

Type 2

(Magazine)

Type 3

(Television)

Present the three advertisements to your classmates and discuss the effectiveness of each with them.

TARGET ACTIVITY

Compare two similar products in a class demonstration. Test them on the basis of claims as stated in collected advertisements about the products. How accurate are the advertised claims?

Product:	**Product:**
Advertised Claims	**Advertised Claims**
Tested Results	**Tested Results**

SPINOFF SELECTIONS

Select one of these topics for further research about advertising.

marketing	psychology	economics	radio
consumer	catalogs	observation	slogans
television	manufacturing	packaging	newspaper
persuasion	propaganda	sensory appeals	

Use this space to record your information.

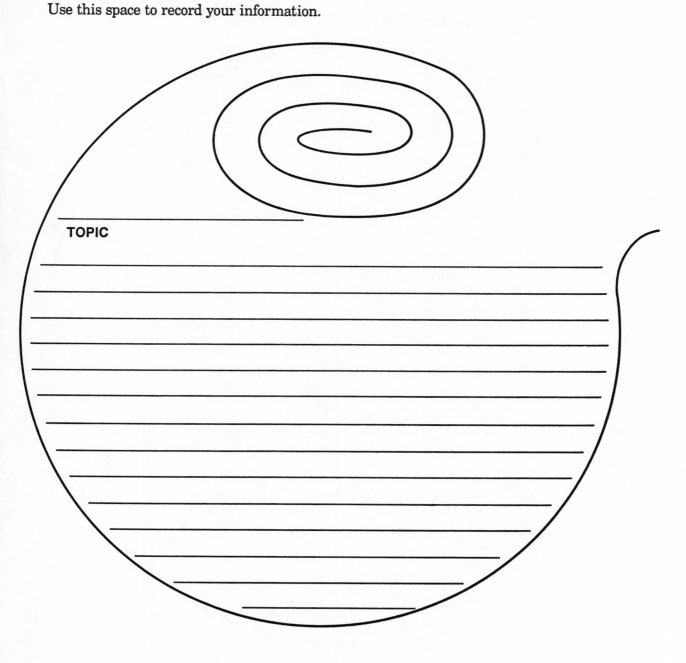

TOPIC

TAKE ACTION

Conduct a survey of at least 30 people of differing age groups. Ask them to name their 5 most memorable ads.

Group their responses in various ways such as:

1. by the type of product mentioned
2. by the most frequently repeated ad
3. by responses from different age groups
4. by the type of technique used in the ad

Use the form below to plan the survey.

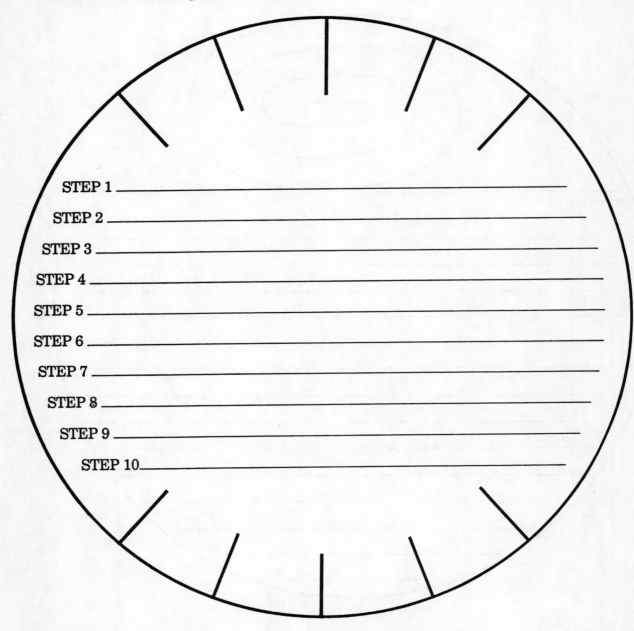

STEP 1 _____

STEP 2 _____

STEP 3 _____

STEP 4 _____

STEP 5 _____

STEP 6 _____

STEP 7 _____

STEP 8 _____

STEP 9 _____

STEP 10 _____

Share the survey results in a letter to a local advertising firm.

CONTRACT

Imagine yourself back in time with the early Greeks and Romans. As you watch struggles among people and with nature, you find yourself wanting explanations about these happenings. You might invent or listen to a myth about how the sun travels across the sky, how the earth is supported in space, why there are seasons, or why we have the personal challenges of sorrow, sickness, and death.

My Target activities will be:

_____

_____

_____

My Spinoffs will be:

_____

_____

_____

I will Take Action by:

_____

_____

_____

My study will begin on _____
Date

My goal is to finish by _____
Date

_____ _____
Student Signature Teacher Signature

TARGET ACTIVITY

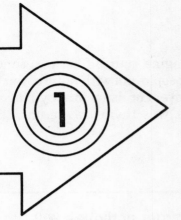

Choose your favorite mythological character. Complete the job application as if you were the chosen character. What other jobs might be suitable for someone with these abilities?

JOB APPLICATION FOR _____

(Occupation or Position)

MYTHOLOGICAL NAME _____

MYTHOLOGICAL PLACE OF RESIDENCE _____

LIST SPECIFIC ABILITIES OR TALENTS THAT APPLY TO THIS JOB.

_____

_____

LIST SPECIFIC TRAINING YOU HAVE RECEIVED THAT WOULD PREPARE YOU FOR THIS JOB.

_____

_____

LIST ANY PEOPLE OR CREATURES THAT WOULD RECOMMEND YOU FOR THIS JOB.

_____

_____

IN YOUR OWN WORDS, TELL WHY YOU WANT THIS JOB.

_____

_____

_____

_____

TARGET ACTIVITY

Choose a myth that you think really teaches a worthwhile lesson. Use puppets as the characters and present this myth to your classmates. Use the checklist below to organize your work.

☐ WRITE THE SCRIPT

☐ DESIGN THE PUPPETS

☐ SELECT PUPPETEERS

☐ CONSTRUCT PUPPETS

☐ DESIGN AND CONSTRUCT SCENERY

☐ LOCATE AND/OR CONSTRUCT PROPS

☐ REHEARSE, REHEARSE, REHEARSE!

☐ ADVERTISE AND PROMOTE

☐ PRESENT AND ENJOY!

Conduct a discussion with your classmates to see if they can think of current situations in which the same lessons can be applied.

TARGET ACTIVITY

As you watch television news or read newspapers, think about major events from the local to the international level. Look for similarities in the myths you read. Explain these similarities in a news commentary.

③

This is a Station MYTH news commentary....

_____

_____

_____

_____

_____

_____

_____

_____

_____

_____

_____

If you enjoyed this type of presentation, see if your teacher would like you to continue matching current events with mythology for the remainder of the year.

TARGET ACTIVITY

Retell your favorite myth in a more up-to-date form. What form will you choose—a newspaper account? a country-western ballad? a television show? a talk show on radio or television?

4

Be sure to include music, costumes, headlines, and the like in your modern-day presentation. Schedule a time with your teacher.

SPINOFF SELECTIONS

Select one of these topics for further research about mythology.

Constellations	Zodiac	American Indian Mythology
Seasons of the year	Zeus	Oriental Mythology
Mount Olympus	Hera	Arachne
Folklore	Pandora	Neptune
Planets	Scandinavian Mythology	Pluto

Use this space to record your information.

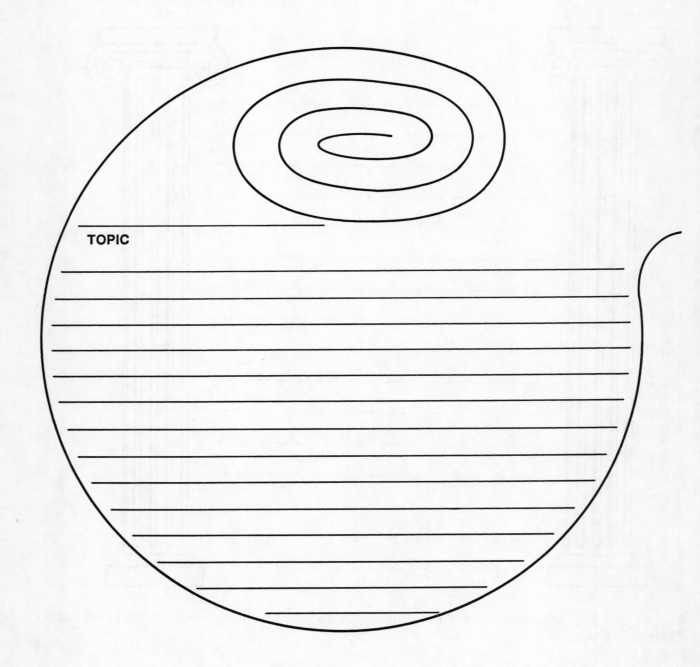

TOPIC

TAKE ACTION

Develop a reading list around certain mythological themes such as seasons, natural events, romance, daring deeds, super challenges, punishments, or heroes/heroines. Use several of the forms below to record your information. Present this list to librarians or teachers as an aid in their planning.

THEME: _____

AUTHOR: _____

TITLE: _____

LIBRARY LOCATION: _____

SUMMARY: _____

_____

_____

_____

_____

CONTRACT

Ichthyology, ornithology, zoology—are they related terms? "Ology" is a suffix used in the English language meaning the study of something. By adding the suffixes, "ist" and "er" to the "ology," you have the name of a person who does this type of study.

My Target activities will be:

_____

_____

_____

My Spinoffs will be:

_____

_____

_____

I will Take Action by:

_____

_____

_____

My study will begin on _____.

Date

My goal is to finish by _____.

Date

_____   _____
Student Signature   Teacher Signature

TARGET ACTIVITY

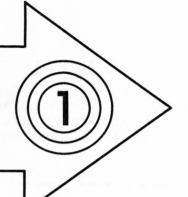

Use a dictionary to describe the topic to be studied in each of the "ologies" listed below. Can you add any more to the list? How many categories can be made from this list?

ANTHROPOLOGY
The study of

_____

CHRONOLOGY
The study of

_____

ETHNOLOGY
The study of

_____

HISTOLOGY
The study of

_____

METHODOLOGY
The study of

_____

NUMEROLOGY
The study of

_____

PHYSIOLOGY
The study of

_____

SPELEOLOGY
The study of

_____

ARCHAEOLOGY
The study of

_____

CRIMINOLOGY
The study of

_____

ETYMOLOGY
The study of

_____

ICHTHYOLOGY
The study of

_____

MICROBIOLOGY
The study of

_____

PALEONTOLOGY
The study of

_____

PSYCHOLOGY
The study of

_____

TOPOLOGY
The study of

_____

BIOLOGY
The study of

_____

CYTOLOGY
The study of

_____

GEOLOGY
The study of

_____

IMMUNOLOGY
The study of

_____

MYTHOLOGY
The study of

_____

PATHOLOGY
The study of

_____

SOCIOLOGY
The study of

_____

ZOOLOGY
The study of

_____

TARGET ACTIVITY

Drop the "y" on each of the studies listed in Target Activity 1 and add "ist" to the word. You now have the name of a person who studies this topic! Make a word search using many of these professions.

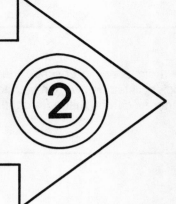

_____   _____   _____

_____   _____   _____

_____   _____   _____

_____   _____   _____

_____   _____   _____

Pretend that you are one or more of these professionals. Where are places in the world that you would find yourself at work?

TARGET ACTIVITY

Compile a list from A to Z of occupations. Each title should end with "ist" or "er". Then carefully choose a descriptive word that will help the reader understand the type of work done by the listed person. Two are already done for you.

Air-borne	A erialist	N	
	B	O	
	C	P	
	D	Q	
Wordy	E tymologist	R	
	F	S	
	G	T	
	H	U	
	I	V	
	J	W	
	K	X	
	L	Y	
	M	Z	

It might be fun to make a book of occupations to share with the librarian and guidance counselor.

TARGET ACTIVITY

Be creative and invent "ology" words to describe the jobs that students, teachers, and other personnel have at school. Write a descriptive story using as many of the new words as possible.

Share this creative word list with your teacher. Maybe these would be good spelling words for the class to tackle.

SPINOFF SELECTIONS

Select one of these topics for further research about "ologies".

branches of science occupations
language/word origins careers
ancient alphabets Daniel Webster
foreign languages William Morris
specialized dictionaries modern alphabet origins

Use this space to record your information.

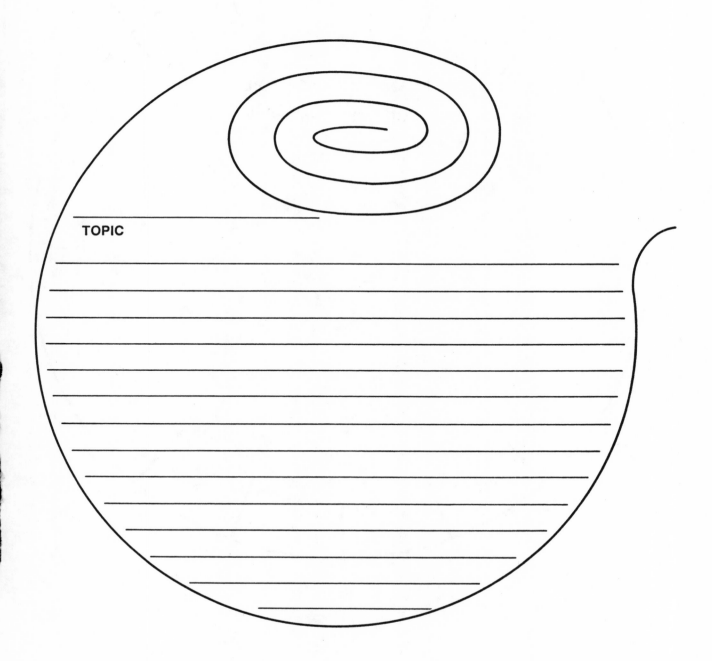

TOPIC

TAKE ACTION

Make some large charts about the most interesting "ologies" that you studied. Be sure to include facts about the type of work this person would do, equipment one would use, training necessary for this career, and places where one might work.

Ask the school librarian or media specialist to display them so other students can learn from the charts.

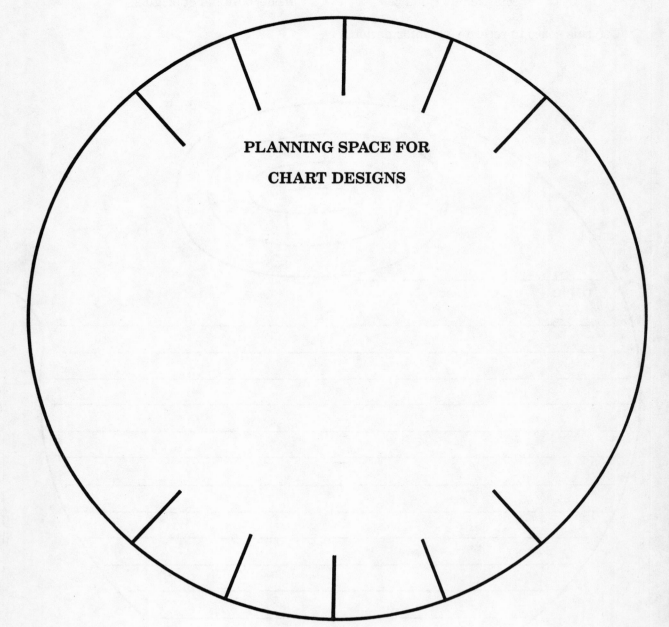

PLANNING SPACE FOR

CHART DESIGNS

CONTRACT

Most of the words ending in "onics" belong to the vocabulary of technology. Physicists, horticulturists, geologists, and doctors are some of the people studying and developing new ideas that will add to our "onics" vocabularies in the near future.

My Target activities will be:

_____
_____
_____

My Spinoffs will be:

_____
_____
_____

I will Take Action by:

_____
_____
_____

My study will begin on _____.
                                      Date

My goal is to finish by _____.
                                      Date

_____   _____
Student Signature   Teacher Signature

TARGET ACTIVITY

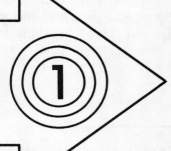

Supersonic jets must break the sound barrier to travel faster than the speed of sound. When they do this, a very loud vibration called a sonic boom occurs. Use a thesaurus to find synonyms for *shake* or *vibrate*.

Synonyms for SHAKE or VIBRATE

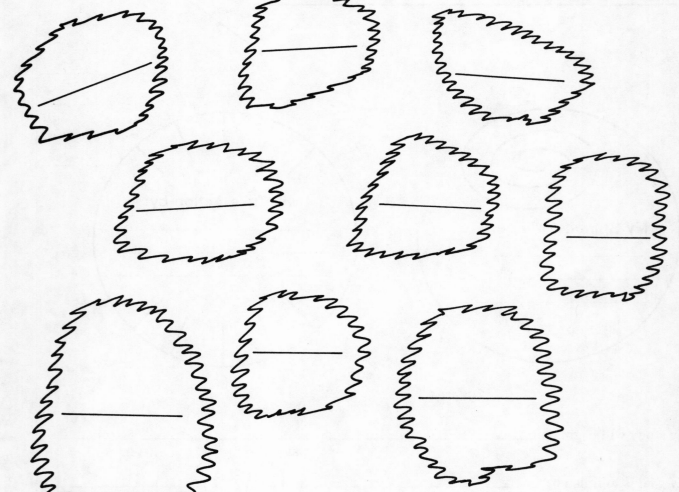

Now, pretend you are near an airport when a sonic boom occurs. For each synonym listed above, name three different things that would shake or vibrate in this way as a result of the sonic boom.

TARGET ACTIVITY

A television show, "The Six Million Dollar Man," made viewers aware of the medical research being done in the field of bionics. Choose 10 verbs and write descriptive sentences to show an increase in speed and/or strength as a result of a bionic replacement.

1. _____

2. _____

3. _____

4. _____

5. _____

6. _____

7. _____

8. _____

9. _____

10. _____

Use one or more of these sentences in an adventure story. Be sure to use synonyms and comparisons to show increased abilities.

TARGET ACTIVITY

Pretend that you are the chief horticulturist aboard a future space station. You are responsible for the production of food from the hydroponic gardens. Complete your journal for the next 5 days; describe the work and the bountiful results.

HORTICULTURAL LOG   STAR DATE _ _ _ _

TARGET ACTIVITY

In mythology, Mnemosyne was the Goddess of Memory. Today, a mnemonic device is a way of helping people remember something. Create some mnemonic devices to help you remember spelling words or other facts.

④

Keys to get you started.

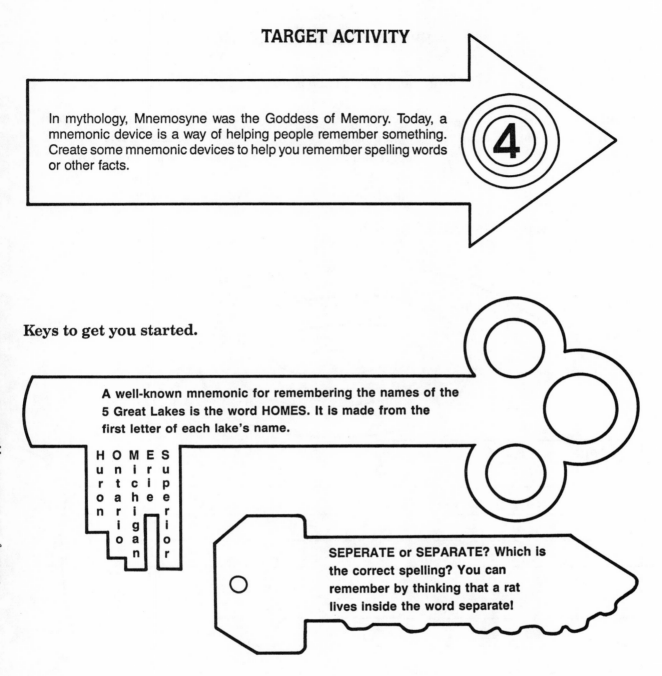

A well-known mnemonic for remembering the names of the 5 Great Lakes is the word HOMES. It is made from the first letter of each lake's name.

H	O	M	E	S
u	n	i	r	u
r	t	c	i	p
o	a	h	e	e
n	r	i		r
	i	g		i
	o	a		o
		n		r

SEPERATE or SEPARATE? Which is the correct spelling? You can remember by thinking that a rat lives inside the word separate!

Create your own memory keys.

Share your mnemonic devices with classmates and have your teacher check on the improvement in your memories.

SPINOFF SELECTIONS

Select one of these topics for further research about "onics".

electronics	acronyms	supersonic transport
plate tectonics	pneumonic	sonic barrier
seismograph	pulmonic	sonic depth finder
astronics	cryogenics	avionics
ionics	nucleonics	sound

Use this space to record your information.

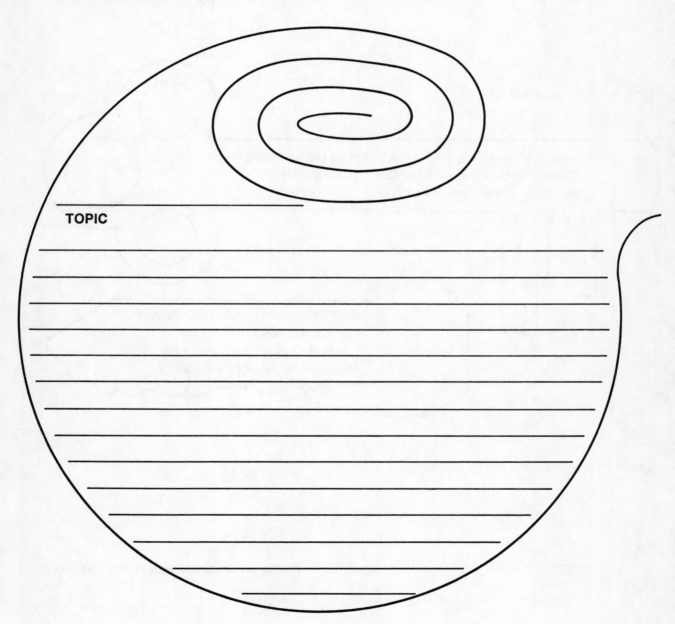

TOPIC

TAKE ACTION

Write a letter to your County Agricultural Extension Office or Farm Bureau to ask for information about hydroponics. If there is a speaker available to demonstrate this method of growing plants, schedule a time with your teacher.

Use the form below to write questions to ask the speaker. (Don't forget to get his/her address and write a thank-you note.)

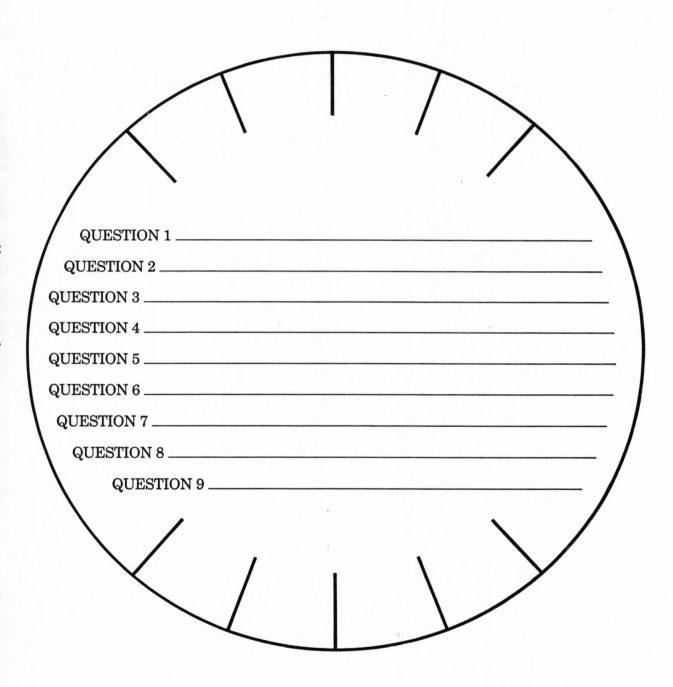

QUESTION 1 _____

QUESTION 2 _____

QUESTION 3 _____

QUESTION 4 _____

QUESTION 5 _____

QUESTION 6 _____

QUESTION 7 _____

QUESTION 8 _____

QUESTION 9 _____

CONTRACT

Palindromes are words, sentences, or number problems that read the same forwards and backwards. For example, radar, noon, and kayak are word palindromes. "Marge lets Norah see Sharon's telegram" is a palindromic sentence. This word pattern is another interesting variation in our language form.

My Target activities will be:

_____

_____

_____

My Spinoffs will be:

_____

_____

_____

I will Take Action by:

_____

_____

_____

My study will begin on _____.

Date

My goal is to finish by _____

Date

_____   _____
Student Signature   Teacher Signature

TARGET ACTIVITY

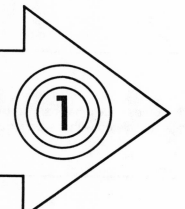

Try a variety of activities with the list of word palindromes below. Alphabetize them, classify them, write a story with them, use rhythm instruments as you spell out the word, and so forth. Have fun!

kayak   toot   level

Hannah   Ada   redder

sis   pep

                                                    ewe

           mum   pup   madam

peep

     noon   dad   wow   Otto

Bob   bib

        noon   eye   Eve

tot

          radar   mom

solos   pop

TARGET ACTIVITY

Palindromes have a back and forth pattern. Try brainstorming several things associated with the patterns listed below.

②

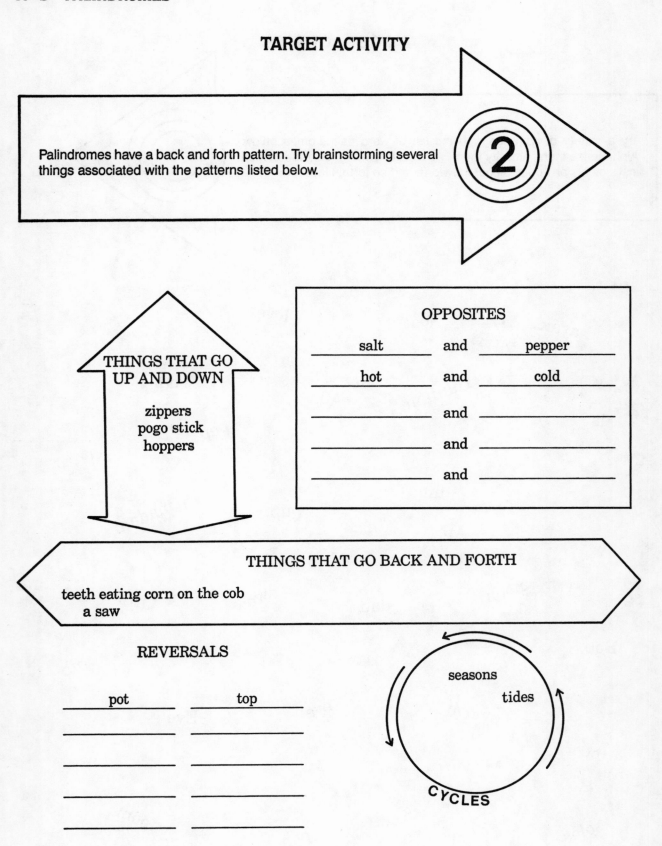

THINGS THAT GO
UP AND DOWN

zippers
pogo stick
hoppers

OPPOSITES

salt	and	pepper
hot	and	cold
	and	
	and	
	and	

THINGS THAT GO BACK AND FORTH

teeth eating corn on the cob
a saw

REVERSALS

pot	top

seasons
tides

CYCLES

Try to write other palindromic sentences, such as this example, "Madam, I'm Adam."

TARGET ACTIVITY

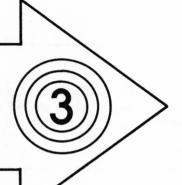

There is a limited supply of word palindromes, so have fun inventing "nonsense" ones of your own. Follow the format below and write some "nonsense" palindromes as correct dictionary entries.

_____ (_____) _____
  entry palindrome   phonetic spelling   part of speech

1._____
                                  definition

_____ (_____) _____
  entry palindrome   phonetic spelling   part of speech

1._____
                                  definition

_____ (_____) _____
  entry palindrome   phonetic spelling   part of speech

1._____
                                  definition

_____ (_____) _____
  entry palindrome   phonetic spelling   part of speech

1._____
                                  definition

_____ (_____) _____
  entry palindrome   phonetic spelling   part of speech

1._____
                                  definition

_____ (_____) _____
  entry palindrome   phonetic spelling   part of speech

1._____
                                  definition

Alphabetize the entries and compile them into a dictionary. Encourage other classmates to create "nonsense" palindromes to add to this dictionary.

TARGET ACTIVITY

Have some calculating fun with number palindromes. Just keep reversing the number order and adding until the sum becomes a palindrome.

One-Step Palindrome

$$+\begin{array}{r}422\\224\end{array}$$

646

Two-Step Palindrome

$$+\begin{array}{r}28\\82\end{array}$$

110

$$+\begin{array}{r}110\\011\end{array}$$

121

TRY THESE!

Three-Step Palindrome

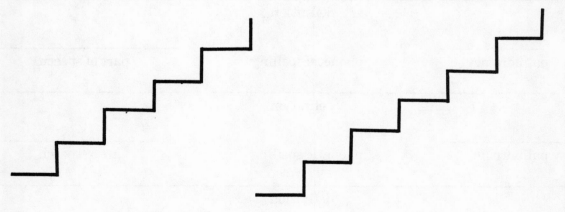

Four-Step Palindrome

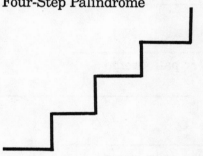

Five-Step Palindrome

Six-Step Palindrome

One of the longest palindromes known is 98 + 89. It takes 24 steps for the palindrome to evolve! Try it out!

SPINOFF SELECTIONS

Select one of these topics for further research about palindromes and other word patterns.

numerical palindromes	acronyms	rebus stories
number patterns	codes	pattern analogies
symmetry	anagrams	synonyms, antonyms, homonyms

Use this space to record your information.

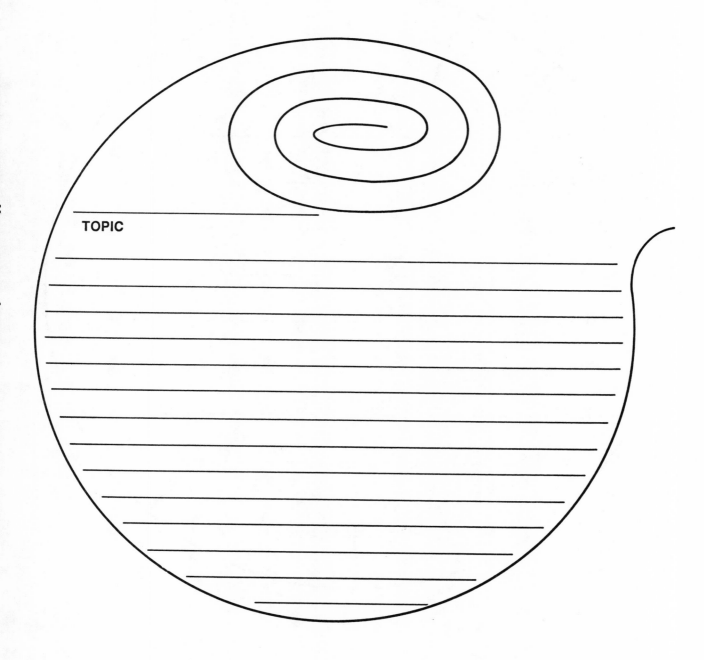

TOPIC

TAKE ACTION

Since palindromes are such unusual and entertaining word patterns, make a palindrome study kit for others to use. Include work from the Target Activities. Take it home and present it to your parents for an "at home fun night."

Use the space below to plan your study kit.

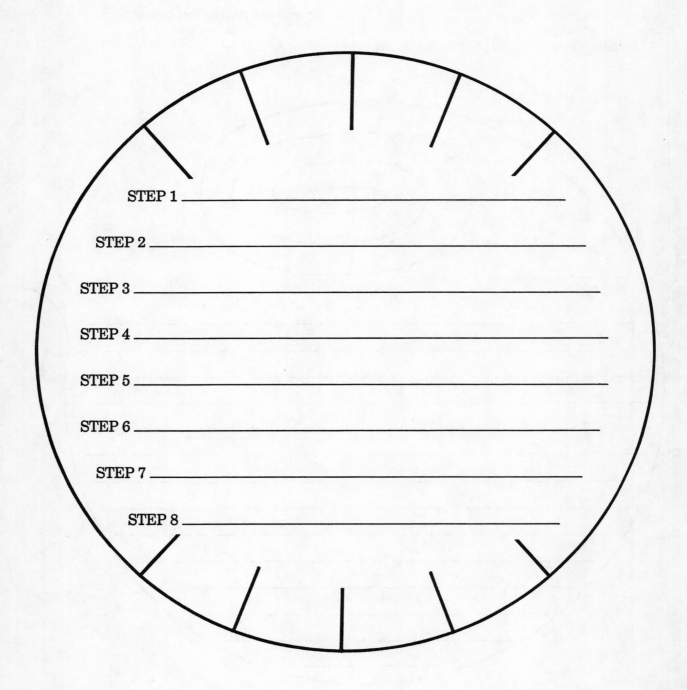

STEP 1 _____

STEP 2 _____

STEP 3 _____

STEP 4 _____

STEP 5 _____

STEP 6 _____

STEP 7 _____

STEP 8 _____

CONTRACT

Do you know people who are afraid of animals? fear heights? dislike dark places? Psychiatrists tell us that phobias are caused when certain fears are experienced again and again. Many times, people can overcome their phobias if they can remember the original incident that produced the fear.

My Target activities will be:

_____
_____
_____

My Spinoffs will be:

_____
_____
_____

I will Take Action by:

_____
_____
_____

My study will begin on _____.
                                                    Date

My goal is to finish by _____.
                                                    Date

_____   _____
Student Signature   Teacher Signature

TARGET ACTIVITY

Eight types of phobias are described below. Use these, or other unusual phobias, to construct a mobile.

1. Acrophobia – fear of high places
2. Agoraphobia – fear of large, open spaces
3. Ailurophobia – fear of cats
4. Claustrophobia – fear of closed-in places
5. Erythrophobia – fear of blushing
6. Triskaidekaphobia – fear of the number 13
7. Xenophobia – fear of strangers or foreigners
8. Zoophobia – fear of animals

Choose geometric shapes for the mobile parts, or be creative and use shapes which relate to the type of phobia being described.

Be sure to include the following on each mobile piece: (1) an illustration or symbols to represent the phobia, (2) a phonetic spelling of the phobia, (3) a definition of the phobia, (4) the actual name of the phobia.

Examples of Creative Shapes

TARGET ACTIVITY

Using the phobias listed in Target Activity 1, brainstorm places, living and nonliving things that people having a type of phobia might want to avoid.

PHOBIA NAME	PLACES TO AVOID	LIVING/NONLIVING THINGS TO AVOID	
		LIVING	NONLIVING

Using the information on the chart above, dramatize these phobias for your classmates and see if they can guess which one you are acting out.

TARGET ACTIVITY

Make up a new phobia. It might be fear of getting a bad report card, of not having a lot of friends, of being shy, and so on. Write a humorous story about experiencing this phobia. Include many descriptive words to help explain and describe your fear and reactions.

Today I _____
_____
_____
_____
_____
_____
_____
_____
_____
_____
_____
_____
_____
_____
_____
_____
_____

TARGET ACTIVITY

Create a word poem about one or more phobias. Keep a dictionary and a thesaurus close at hand.

ERYTHROPHOBIA...

> Embarrassed
>
> Reddening
>
> Yielding to emotion;
>
> Timid
>
> Heated
>
> Response, too noticeable to
>
> Overlook.
>
> ...a fear of blushing!

SPINOFF SELECTIONS

Select one of these topics for further research about phobias:

psychology	counseling	therapy
psychiatry	sociology	reactions
mental health	parapsychology	nervous system

Use this space to record your information.

TOPIC

TAKE ACTION

Make up a questionnaire to give your classmates about phobias they may have. Then invite the school psychologist to speak to your classmates about methods to counteract common fears and nervousness.

Use the form below to plan the questionnaire and questions you would like to ask the school psychologist.

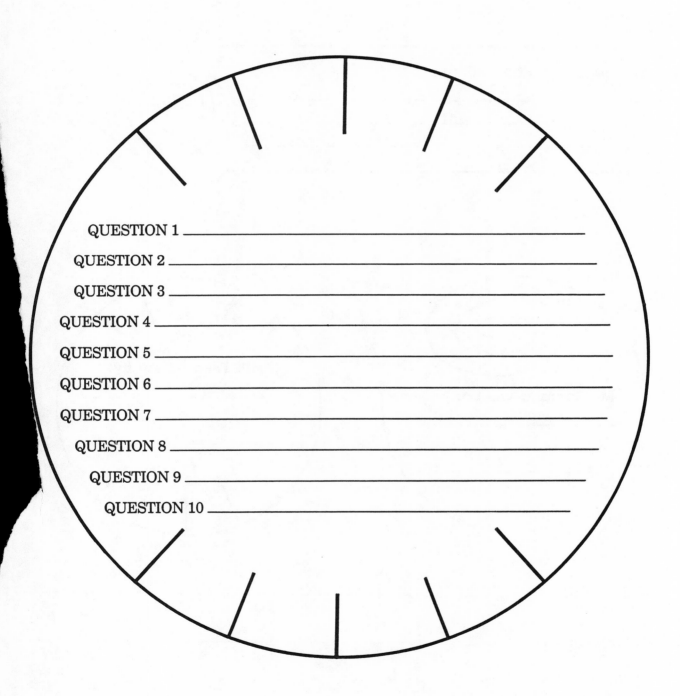

QUESTION 1 _____

QUESTION 2 _____

QUESTION 3 _____

QUESTION 4 _____

QUESTION 5 _____

QUESTION 6 _____

QUESTION 7 _____

QUESTION 8 _____

QUESTION 9 _____

QUESTION 10 _____

CONTRACT

"Sing me a rainbow" and Somewhere over the rainbow" are both well-known lyrics from popular songs about everyone's favorite thing—a rainbow. That arc of color painted across the sky after a rain has always captured the imagination. How does it get there? Is there really a pot of gold at the end?

My Target activities will be:
_____
_____
_____

My Spinoffs will be:
_____
_____
_____

I will Take Action by:
_____
_____
_____

My study will begin on _____.
Date

My goal is to finish by _____.
Date

_____   _____
Student Signature   Teacher Signature

TARGET ACTIVITY

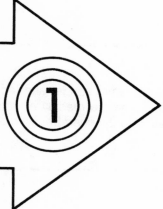

Roy G. Biv is a name used as a memory device to list the order in which colors appear in the rainbow. Create a cartoon character for this name and write a comic strip that explains the rainbow origin of his name.

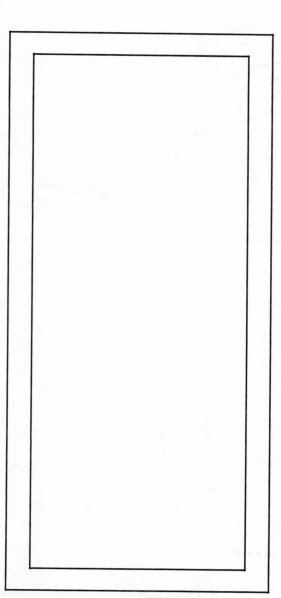

Roy G. Biv

TARGET ACTIVITY

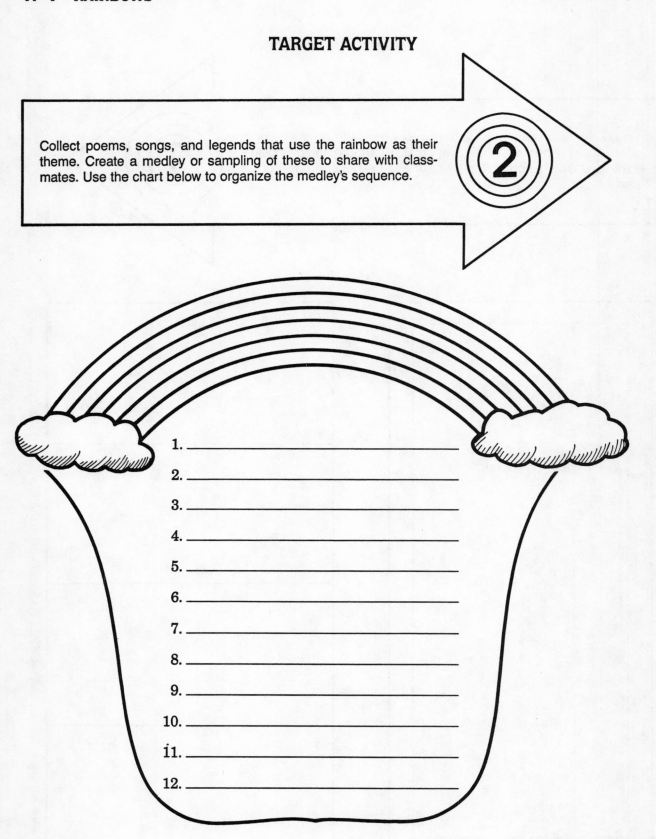

Collect poems, songs, and legends that use the rainbow as their theme. Create a medley or sampling of these to share with class-mates. Use the chart below to organize the medley's sequence.

②

1. _____
2. _____
3. _____
4. _____
5. _____
6. _____
7. _____
8. _____
9. _____
10. _____
11. _____
12. _____

Write a fictional explanation for the formation of a rainbow. Perhaps you could use a character from Greek mythology, a holiday character, or a character from fiction.

TARGET ACTIVITY

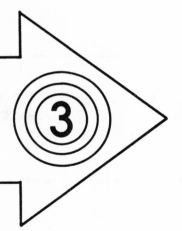

Make a poster that diagrams the formation of a rainbow in the sky. Prepare a speech that will inform an audience about this process. Use the poster as a visual aid.

SPEECH TITLE: _____

PURPOSE OF SPEECH: _____

_____

_____

ATTENTION GETTER: _____

_____

_____

TEXT OUTLINE: _____

_____

_____

_____

_____

_____

_____

_____

_____

_____

CLOSING STATEMENT: _____

_____

   Is a rain shower the only way to produce a rainbow? Do some research in science books and encyclopedias to find other methods. Demonstrate one or more of these during the speech.

TARGET ACTIVITY

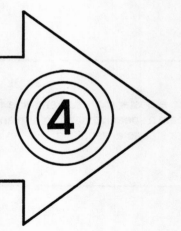

An analogy is a comparison that helps someone understand or visualize an idea more easily. Using the rainbow's colors, shape, origin, and legends as a theme, write some creative comparisons.

A RAINBOW IS TO _____ AS A _____

IS TO _____ , BECAUSE _____

_____ .

THE RAINBOW'S STRIPES ARE TO _____

AS THE _____ ARE TO _____ ,

BECAUSE _____ .

_____ IS TO THE ARC OF A RAINBOW AS

A _____ IS TO _____ ,

BECAUSE _____ .

_____ IS TO _____

AS A POT OF GOLD IS TO THE END OF THE RAINBOW, BECAUSE _____

_____ .

_____ IS TO _____

AS _____ IS TO _____

BECAUSE _____ .

_____ IS TO _____

AS _____ IS TO _____

BECAUSE _____ .

_____ IS TO _____

SPINOFF SELECTIONS

Select one of these topics for further research about rainbows.

refraction	Sir Isaac Newton	optics	mirage
prism	Northern Lights	light	color
spectrum	reflection	corona	

Use this space to record your information.

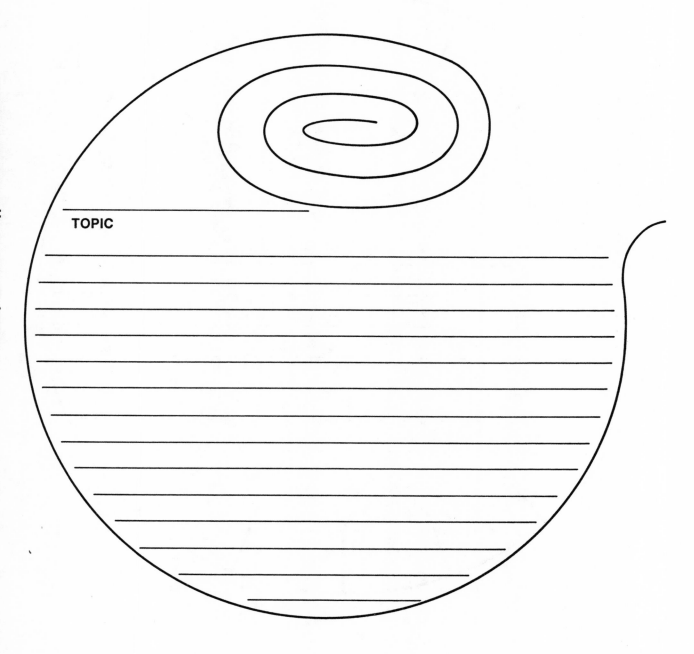

TOPIC

TAKE ACTION

Many products in catalogs and stores use the rainbow design or variations of it. Make a collage or display of some products and/or pictures of them. How many people in your class have one of these products? Why did they choose it?

Design a new product of your own using a rainbow theme. Create an advertisement to "sell it" to your classmates. Use the form below to plan a product and advertisement.

Words in Print

LIBRARY PROJECTS

V–1   Books and Printing Through the Ages
V–2   Classics
V–3   Fairy Tales, Fables, Folk Tales
V–4   Famous Libraries
V–5   Magazines
V–6   Newbery and Caldecott Award Winners
V–7   Poets and Poetry

CONTRACT

Bones, cave walls, wood, papyrus, fabric, and parchment made from animal skins were the first media on which early man began recording written symbols and pictures. As cultural groups began to form communities, and inventions such as paper and the printing press became widely used, our love for and dependence on books has continued. Can you even imagine a world today without books?

My Target activities will be:

_____

_____

_____

My Spinoffs will be:

_____

_____

_____

I will Take Action by:

_____

_____

_____

My study will begin on _____ .

Date

My goal is to finish by _____ .

Date

_____   _____

Student Signature   Teacher Signature

TARGET ACTIVITY

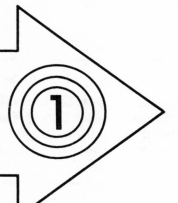

Printing on clay tablets proved to be a long-lasting method of recording cultural information. Thousands of tablets from the Sumerian civilization were discovered in the 1850s. Record facts about these "books" on clay tablets of your design.

TOPICS TO CONSIDER
FOR FACT GATHERING

- Symbols used on tablets
- Keys used to break the symbol codes
- Archaeologist(s) who made discoveries of these tablets
- Location(s) of discoveries
- Description of collections
- Sumerian Culture
- King Sennacherib of Assyria

TARGET ACTIVITY

Paper was thought to be invented by the Chinese around 105 A.D. The art of making paper then spread throughout Baghdad, Egypt, and Europe during the next 1000 years. Use the following method to make paper and inscribe a message using a calligraphic technique.

RECYCLED PAPER

1. Tear newspaper, construction paper, or other types of paper into strips or squares. Adjust color as you blend.

2. Add small pieces of paper to a blender that is half full of water.

3. Blend on high speed until a "mush" is formed. You may add bits of yarn or ribbon to this mixture. The blend needs to be a thick consistency.

4. Pour the mixture into a dishpan half full of water and swirl the water so that the fiber will be suspended.

5. Quickly slip a piece of window screen (6-8″ square) under the suspended fiber.

6. Bring the screen up through the water so that fibers are caught on top of the screen.

7. Lay the fiber-covered screen on folded newspaper to drain for an hour.

8. Place the fiber-covered screen between two pieces of manila paper and iron to remove the remaining dampness. Cool paper frequently.

9. After the paper is dry, gently lift the edges from the screen, and peel it off.

10. Leave the edges ragged for a more textured writing surface, or trim them for a more uniform shape.

TARGET ACTIVITY

During the Middle Ages, Christian monks labored for years in scriptoria to copy, illuminate, and bind books. Investigate techniques used by these monks, and then produce a 5- to 10-page book using similar methods.

Plan the pages of your book before you begin.

After "printing this book, prepare a speech to convince library users to take better care of the expensive reference books and/or one-of-a-kind books housed in the library.

TARGET ACTIVITY

Johannes Gutenberg of Germany is credited with the invention of a printing process of movable type. Following this invention in the 1400s, increasing demands for knowledge and books led to an information explosion that is still occurring today.

Use a branching diagram or brainstorming web to illustrate the widespread effect of Gutenberg's printing process.

GUTENBERG'S PRINTING PRESS

SPINOFF SELECTIONS

Select one of these topics for further research about Books and Printing Through the Ages.

Johannes Gutenberg	Linotype	Bibliophile
John Peter Zenger	Photocopying	Rare books
Currier & Ives	Offset	Calligraphy
Engraving	Typewriter	Papermaking
Block Printing	Word Processor	Newspaper Careers
Silk Screen Printing	Book Binding	

Use this space to record your information.

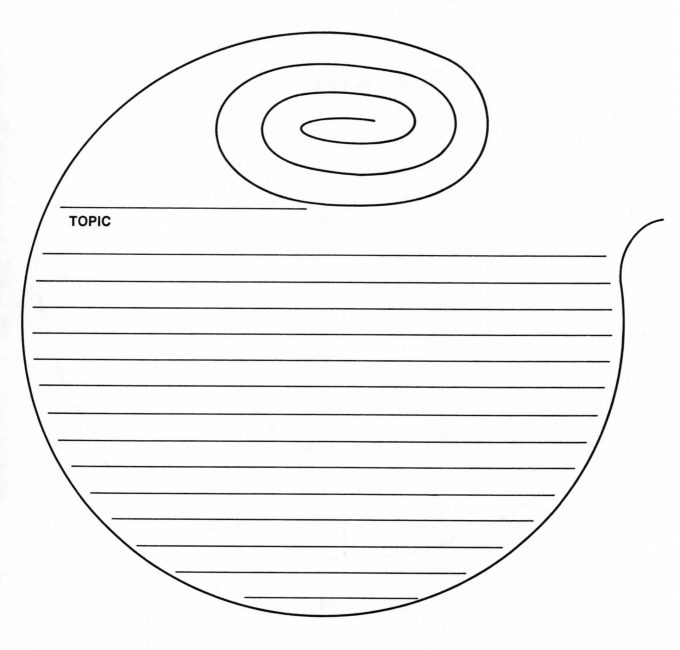

TOPIC

TAKE ACTION

Visit a modern print shop and observe the methods used to reproduce written and graphic materials in mass quantities. Use the form below to list questions to ask during the visit.

The classified section of the telephone book is a good source for print shops. Call for an appointment, and be sure to write a thank-you letter after the visit.

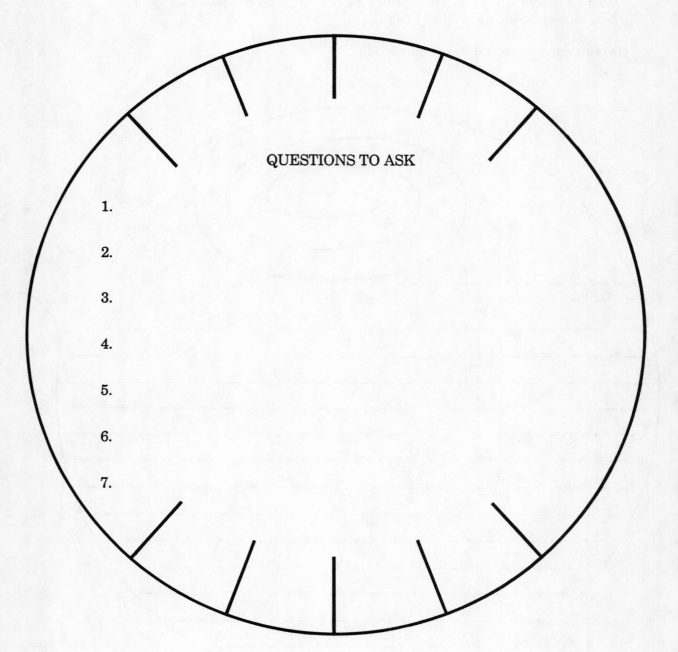

QUESTIONS TO ASK

1.

2.

3.

4.

5.

6.

7.

CONTRACT

Since early times, written expression has contained the qualities of feeling, experience, and imagination. These elements, used to create fine literature or classics, have survived the passage of time throughout the world and serve as permanent models for others to emulate. Although we live in the present, we are transported to other places and times through the powerful magic of literary classics.

My Target activities will be:

_____

_____

_____

My Spinoffs will be:

_____

_____

_____

I will Take Action by:

_____

_____

_____

My study will begin on _____
                                                    Date

My goal is to finish by _____
                                                    Date

_____   _____
Student Signature   Teacher Signature

TARGET ACTIVITY

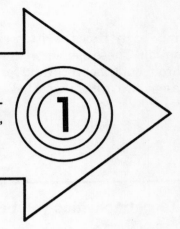

Is your reading preference mystery? adventure? science fiction? Literary classics can be found in any category. Select a classic from the list, find it in the library, check it out and start reading!

MYSTERY

Bronte, Charlotte – *Jane Eyre*
Doyle, Sir Arthur Conan – *The Hound of the Baskervilles*
Hugo, Victor – *The Hunchback of Notre Dame*
Poe, Edgar Allan – *The Pit and the Pendulum*

ADVENTURE

Defoe, Daniel – *Robinson Crusoe*
Dickens, Charles – *A Tale of Two Cities*
London, Jack – *The Call of the Wild*
Melville, Herman – *Moby Dick*
Stevenson, Robert Louis – *Kidnapped*
Verne, Jules – *Around the World in Eighty Days*

SCIENCE FICTION

Shelley, Mary – *Frankenstein*
Verne, Jules – *Journey to the Center of the Earth*
Wells, H.G. – *The Time Machine*
Wells, H.G. – *The War of the Worlds*

OTHER — GENERAL

Crane, Stephen – *The Red Badge of Courage*
Dickens, Charles – *Oliver Twist*
Spyri, Johanna – *Heidi*

TARGET ACTIVITY

Who is the author of the classic you are reading? Do some research and find out about his/her life. *Summarize* your findings in the "bio boxes."

BIO BOX SUMMARY

Book: _____ Author: _____ (Born _____ Died _____) Country of Origin: _____ Draw a symbol that would represent his/her life:	Briefly summarize the family life and education of the author.
List five important personal or world events that might have affected the writing of the author.	List other works by this same author.

Describe how the author's life and times might have directly influenced the classic you are reading.

TARGET ACTIVITY

Which character of the classic you are reading would you like to meet? Why? What questions would you ask if you were able to spend a day together? How might you entertain this character? Describe your experiences in a story.

The Day_____Came to Visit

_____

_____

_____

_____

_____

_____

_____

_____

_____

_____

_____

_____

_____

_____

_____

_____

TARGET ACTIVITY

Pretend that you are a movie tycoon getting ready to produce the classic you are reading. Which actors and actresses might be hired for the leading roles? What personality qualities would make them appropriate for the characters? What type of advertisement would attract the public to see the film?

Examine film advertisements in the local newspaper for ideas. Design an ad for this film.

SPINOFF SELECTIONS

FIND OUT ABOUT THE LIFE OF: OR   **READ THE CLASSIC:**

Louisa May Alcott
James Fenimore Cooper
Washington Irving
Henry Wadsworth Longfellow
Samuel Clemens
Thomas Paine
Rudyard Kipling
Nathaniel Hawthorne

Black Beauty
Gulliver's Travels
The Last of the Mohicans
The Man in the Iron Mask
The Three Musketeers
Treasure Island
Wuthering Heights

Use this space to record your information.

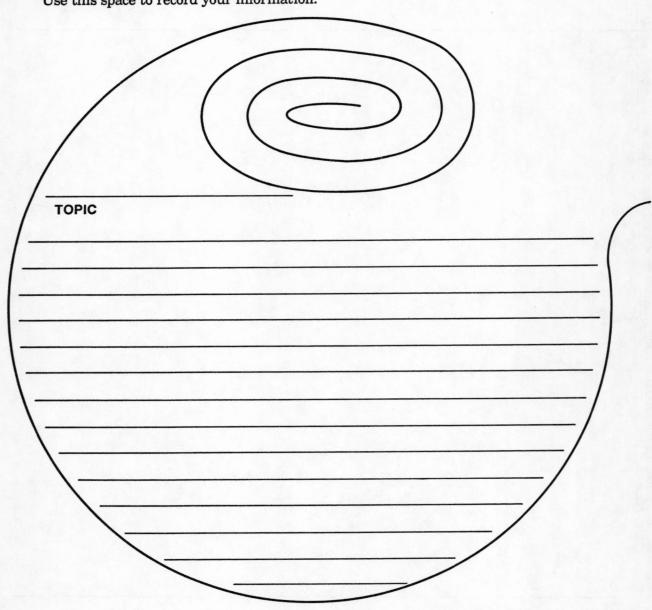

TOPIC

TAKE ACTION

Many public libraries and/or museums have film collections based on classics. Call and conduct a telephone survey. Ask about available films and procedures for checking them out. Compile a list for teachers to use. Display it in your school library. It might be possible to arrange with the PTA to have a "classic film night." Check with your school administrator to see if this would be possible.

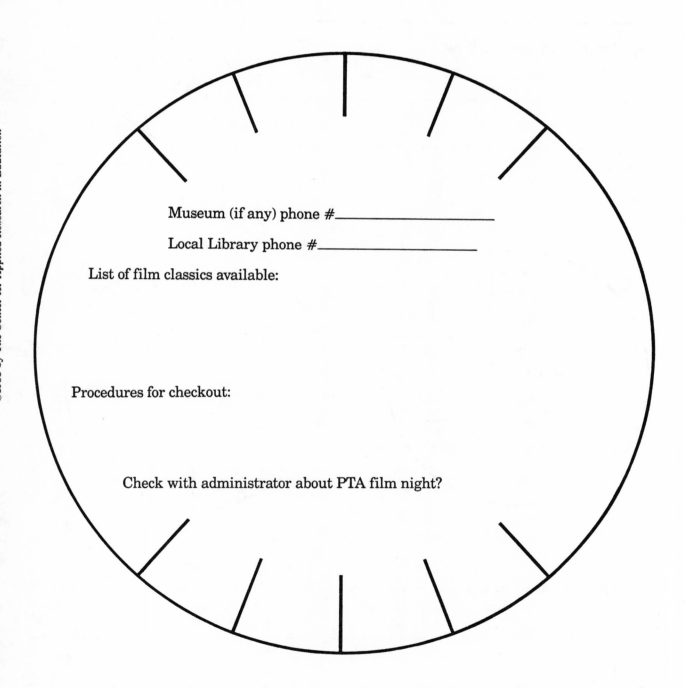

Museum (if any) phone #_____

Local Library phone #_____

List of film classics available:

Procedures for checkout:

Check with administrator about PTA film night?

CONTRACT

Enchantment, good versus evil, colorful characters, lessons to consider, and grand exaggeration are all qualities a reader will find in literary tales and fables. Folk literature has always been a part of every race's heritage and will probably continue to be as long as a storyteller is around!

My Target activities will be:

_____

_____

_____

My Spinoffs will be:

_____

_____

_____

I will Take Action by:

_____

_____

_____

My study will begin on _____ .

Date

My goal is to finish by _____ .

Date

_____   _____
Student Signature   Teacher Signature

TARGET ACTIVITY

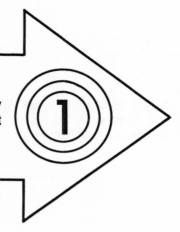

Change or transformation from a realistic setting or actions to fantasy is the basic story line used in writing fairy tales. Name fairy tales that are examples of those types of changes from real-life to fantasy.

Fairy tales that change a realistic setting and action into a fantasy situation are:

Example: *The Lion, the Witch, and the Wardrobe*

Fairy tales in which a character is transformed from one type to another, and then requires a special action to change back are:

Example: "Beauty and the Beast"

Design some illustrations to show the moment when real life changes to fantasy in one of these stories.

TARGET ACTIVITY

Many fairy tales of olden times use a character arrangement of the number 3. Make a 3's mobile naming several stories and the trio of characters involved in the plots.

②

EXAMPLE:

3 StepSisters & Cinderella

TARGET ACTIVITY

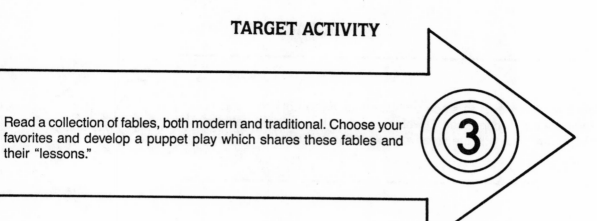

Read a collection of fables, both modern and traditional. Choose your favorites and develop a puppet play which shares these fables and their "lessons."

DESIGN A PLAYBILL TO ADVERTISE YOUR FABLE-RAMA.

TARGET ACTIVITY

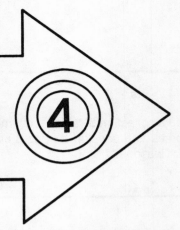

Folk tales have existed since prehistoric times to entertain and to explain natural occurrences. Develop a science lesson that combines present-day facts with the creative explanation of a folk tale.

HINT: ● Seasons of the year, echoes, lightning and thunder, and the sunrise/sunset of a day are all explained in Greek or Roman mythology.
     ● The creation of the Great Lakes, the Grand Canyon, and the extremely high tides in the Bay of Fundy are all credited to Paul Bunyan in various tall tales.

LESSON PLAN TO TEACH _____

USING THE FOLK TALE, _____ .

SCIENCE TERMS	STORY CHARACTERS, SETTING, PLOT

LESSON SEQUENCE

LESSON EVALUATION

SPINOFF SELECTIONS

Select one of these topics for further research about Fairy tales, Fables, and Folk tales.

Aesop's Fables
Greek and Roman Mythology
Norse Mythology
superstitions
International Folk Tales
The Brothers Grimm
fairies, pixies, elves
tall tales

Hans Christian Anderson
C.S. Lewis
E.B. White
Maurice Sendak
Joel Chandler Harris
Charles Perrault
Joseph Jacobs
J.R. Tolkien

Use this space to record your information.

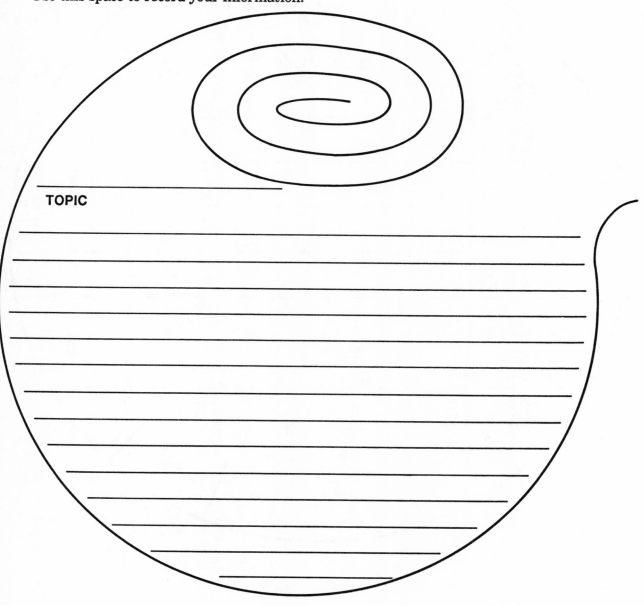

TOPIC

TAKE ACTION

Fairy tales, folk tales, and fables have been illustrated, reprinted, and retold in a variety of ways. Make a library display showing many variations of your favorite stories. Include books, dolls, souvenirs, magazines, films and filmstrips, records, and so forth, in the display. Keep a record of borrowed items on the form below.

LIBRARY DISPLAY

ITEM:
LOANED BY: _____

ITEM:
LOANED BY: _____

ITEM:
LOANED BY: _____

ITEM:
LOANED BY: _____

ITEM:
LOANED BY: _____

ITEM:
LOANED BY: _____

ITEM:
LOANED BY: _____

ITEM:
LOANED BY: _____

CONTRACT

The Latin word, *liber*, meaning book, became the root of the library of the past—a building for large collections of books. Today's libraries offer information in many forms and services of every variety. Sharing is the real purpose of a library, and most of us enjoy and receive that service free of charge! Modern day libraries are constantly undergoing change to meet the challenges and demands of today's technology-oriented users.

My Target activities will be:

_____
_____
_____

My Spinoffs will be:

_____
_____
_____

I will Take Action by:

_____
_____
_____

My study will begin on _____.

Date

My goal is to finish by _____.

Date

_____   _____
Student Signature   Teacher Signature

TARGET ACTIVITY

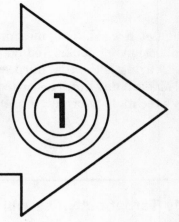

Libraries that have existed for a century or more can truly be described as treasure chests of knowledge. Choose a famous library from the Spinoff Section and investigate the history and collections it houses. Create a display "chest" to share this "wealth."

DISPLAY SUGGESTIONS:

1. Use the library's architectural features to design the outside of the chest.
2. Design symbols to represent major collections housed in the library.
3. Illustrate important details on each of these symbols.
4. Place the collection fact symbols inside the library chest.
5. Display your work so that others may learn about this famous library.

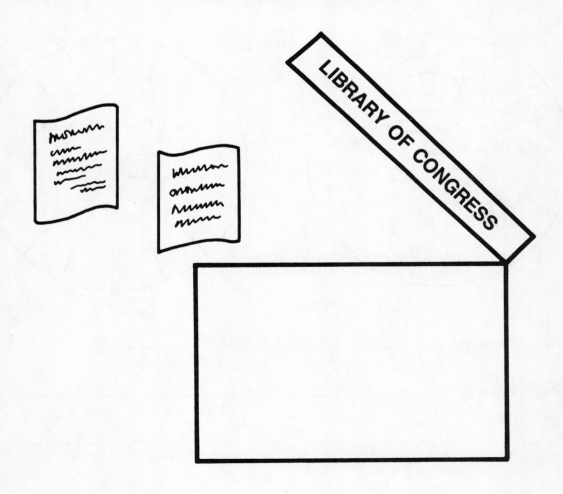

TARGET ACTIVITY

People in the early civilizations of Egypt, Mesopotamia, Greece, and Rome developed libraries of clay tablets and papyrus or animal skin scrolls. Illustrate the history and purpose of these libraries in a time line mural.

②

Be sure to include some of these topics in the mural.

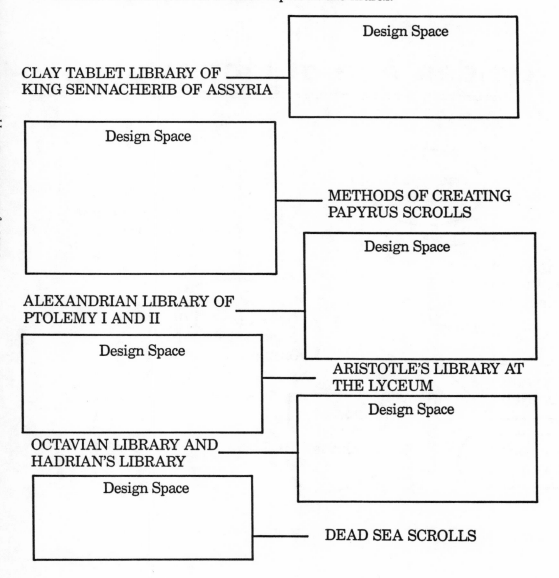

Design Space

CLAY TABLET LIBRARY OF ——————
KING SENNACHERIB OF ASSYRIA

Design Space

————— METHODS OF CREATING
PAPYRUS SCROLLS

Design Space

ALEXANDRIAN LIBRARY OF —————
PTOLEMY I AND II

Design Space

————— ARISTOTLE'S LIBRARY AT
THE LYCEUM

Design Space

OCTAVIAN LIBRARY AND —————
HADRIAN'S LIBRARY

Design Space

————— DEAD SEA SCROLLS

TARGET ACTIVITY

The centuries of 1600 and 1700 are referred to as the "Golden Age of Libraries." Incorporate the topic ideas below into a mobile design that illustrates major events of the "Golden Age."

Golden Age of Libraries

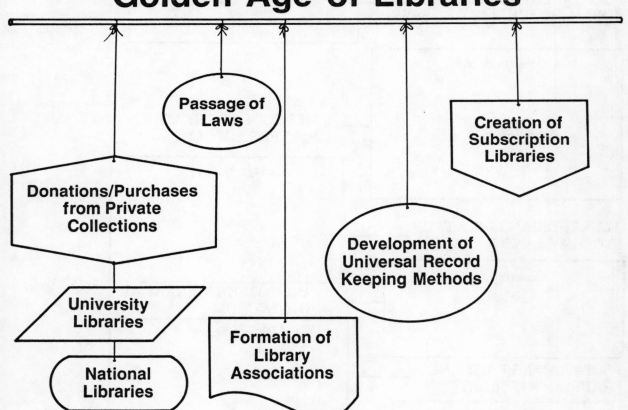

Passage of Laws

Creation of Subscription Libraries

Donations/Purchases from Private Collections

Development of Universal Record Keeping Methods

University Libraries

National Libraries

Formation of Library Associations

TARGET ACTIVITY

Modern school and public libraries have A to Z offerings for their users. Visit an area library and discover the variety of available offerings and opportunities by completing this A to Z list.

A _____	N _____
B _____	O _____
C _____	P _____
D _____	Q _____
E _____	R _____
F _____	S _____
G _____	T _____
H _____	U _____
I _____	V _____
J _____	W _____
K _____	X _____
L _____	Y _____
M _____	Z _____

SPINOFF SELECTIONS

Select one of these topics for further research about Famous Libraries.

National Library of Canada
Library of Parliament, Canada
British Library, London
Bibliothèque Nationale, Paris
Vatican Library
Jagiellonian University, Poland
Lenin State Library, Moscow
Egyptian National Library, Cairo
Jewish National and University
   Library, Jerusalem

Library of Congress
Delhi Public Library, India
National Library of Australia
International Federation of Library
   Association and Institutions
Folger Shakespeare Library
Library Careers
Melvil Dewey
Andrew Carnegie

Use this space to record your information.

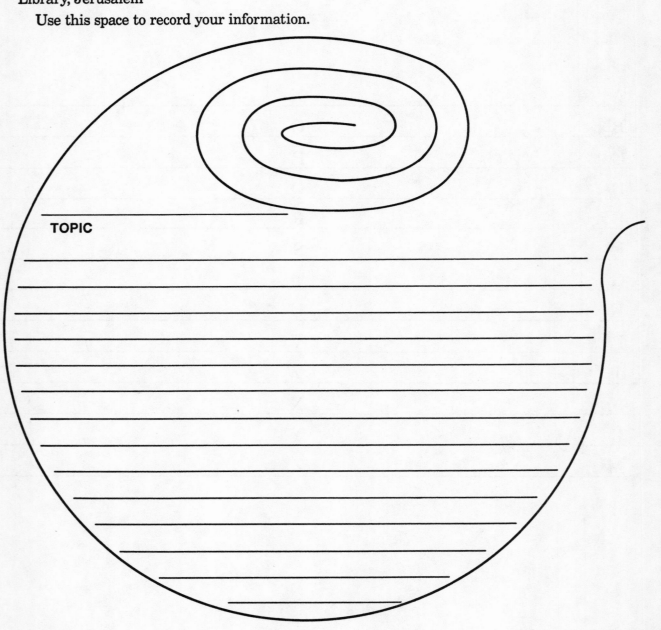

TOPIC

TAKE ACTION

Throughout the centuries, the physical design, content, services, and working atmosphere of the library has been changed to meet the needs of each society of users. Consider the plan and function of your present-day school or public library. Then, design changes that you predict will be necessary for a society of users 80 years from now.

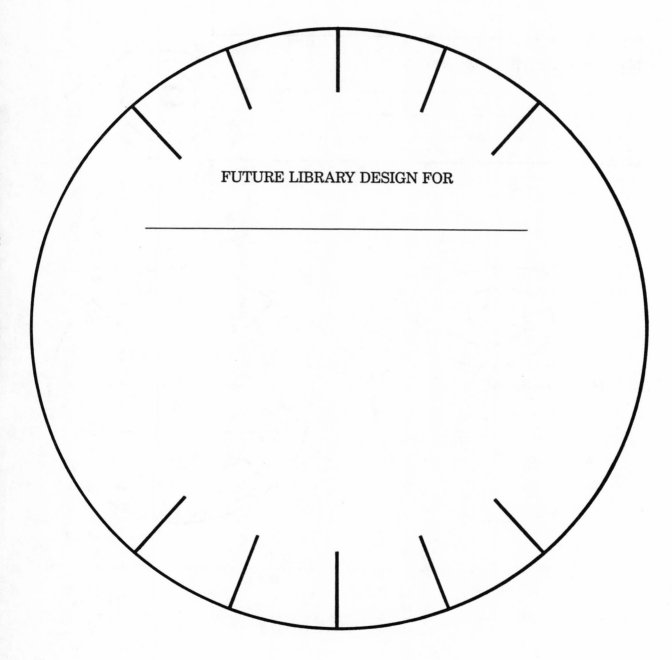

FUTURE LIBRARY DESIGN FOR

_____

CONTRACT

Magazines, periodicals, and journals are materials published at regular intervals during the course of a year. The earliest known appeared in the 18th century.

This special type of reading matter can be found for most hobbies, interests, or age groups. Many magazines have published the work of some of the greatest writers and illustrators of the time. We can be informed and entertained by reading through this type of publication.

My Target activities will be:

_____

_____

_____

My Spinoffs will be:

_____

_____

_____

I will Take Action by:

_____

_____

My study will begin on _____.
Date

My goal is to finish by _____.
Date

_____
Student Signature

_____
Teacher Signature

TARGET ACTIVITY

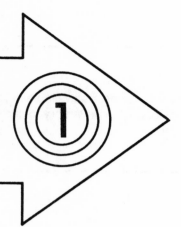

Make a time line tracing the development of magazines. Record the year, magazine name, and a few words about its contents. (You may trace this information for the United States, Canada, Great Britain, or France.)

COUNTRY: _____

1700s --

1800s --

1900s --

TARGET ACTIVITY

What magazines are available in your school library for students your age? Conduct an inventory to find out. A few have been done to start you off.

LIBRARY INVENTORY OF MAGAZINES SUBSCRIBED TO

NAME OF MAGAZINE	CONTENTS DESCRIPTION	PLACE OF PUBLICATION
National Geographic World	games, puzzles, photojournalism	Washington, D.C.
Stone Soup	literary; written and illustrated entirely by children	Santa. Cruz, California
Owl	articles and activities dealing with nature	Toronto, Ontario

TARGET ACTIVITY

Advertisements are an important part of the financial well-being of magazines. By using catchy words, phrases, illustrations, the reader's attention is captured in an attempt to sell products. Find a magazine that you have permission to cut. Create a collage of the attention-getting language used.

ADVERTISEMENT COLLAGE

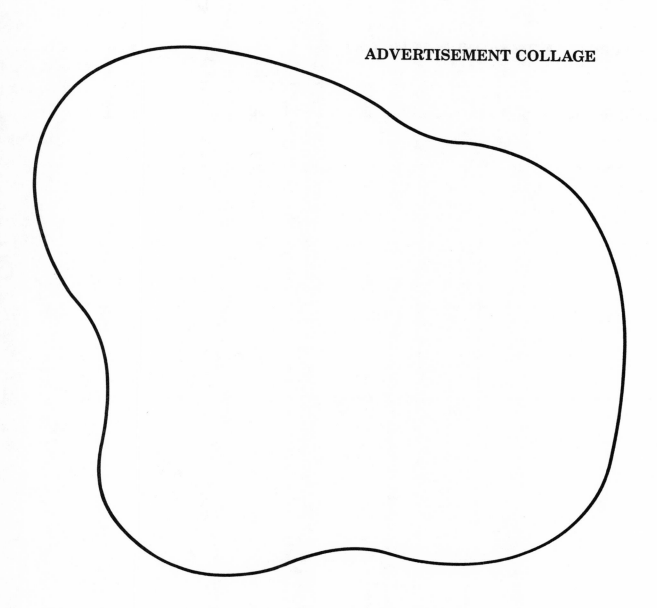

How do these ads differ from those found in magazines for children?

TARGET ACTIVITY

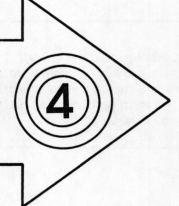

Many children's magazines will publish student's work. Write a story or poem; create an interesting puzzle or brainteaser; take some unusual photos. Select a magazine from Target 2 that has material in it similar to what you are doing. Send your contribution to the editorial office. Find the address on the inside front cover or Table of Contents page.

MY CREATIVE IDEA TO SUBMIT WILL BE:

_____

(Use this space to plan what you will submit to the publishers.)

SPINOFF SELECTIONS

Select one of these topics for further research about magazines.

Marshall Field
Benjamin Franklin
John Peter Zenger
William Randolph Hearst
Joseph Pulitzer
Committee of correspondence

The Penny Press
Poor Richard's Almanac
Tabloids
comics/cartoons
The Tatler
Godey's Lady's Book

journalism
early newspapers
early magazines
foreign magazines
advertising
radio/TV

Use this space to record your information.

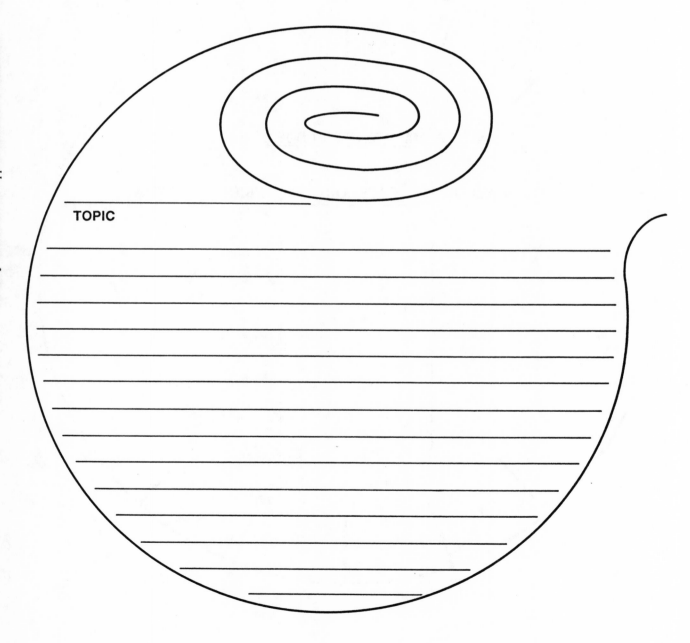

TOPIC

TAKE ACTION

Visit a place near your home where magazines are sold, and do some browsing. Find magazines in different categories for students your age of varied interests. How do they compare in price? What rating would be appropriate for their educational value? Which would you enjoy most? least?

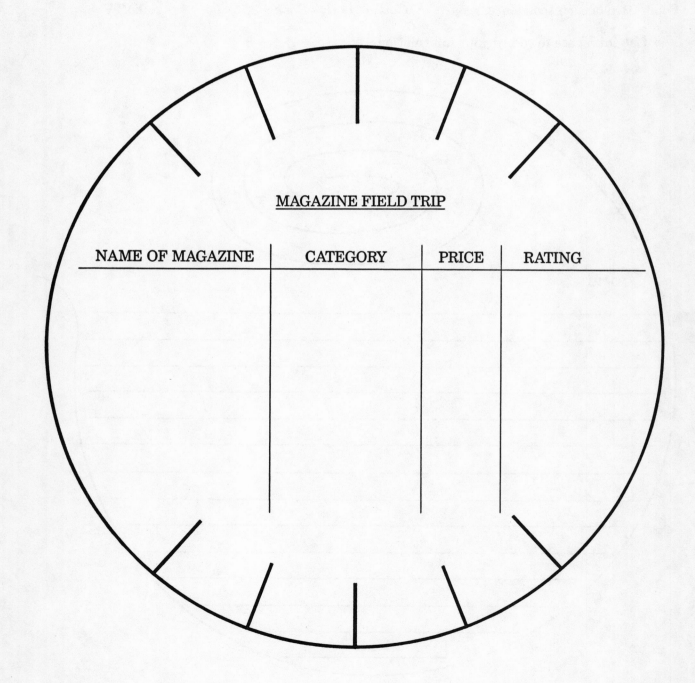

MAGAZINE FIELD TRIP

NAME OF MAGAZINE	CATEGORY	PRICE	RATING

CONTRACT

Excellence in literature for children is recognized each year through special awards that were originally intended to motivate authors to create high-quality literature. The Newbery Medal and Caldecott Award books represent the finest available for young readers, and might be called contemporary "classics."

The Newbery Medal was named for John Newbery (1713-1767), a well-known English publisher who created a book especially for children. Small enough for a young child to hold, *A Little Pretty Pocket Book* was the first of many he published.

My Target activities will be:

_____

_____

_____

My Spinoffs will be:

_____

_____

_____

I will Take Action by:

_____

_____

_____

My study will begin on _____.
Date

My goal is to finish by _____.
Date

_____   _____
Student Signature   Teacher Signature

TARGET ACTIVITY

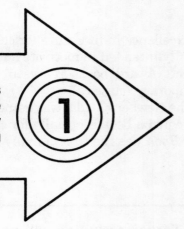

The Newbery Medal, established by Frederic G. Melcher in 1921, is presented each year by the American Library Association. Use the card catalogue in the library and browse through some of the Newbery Award books. Select one to read using the list below as a starting guide.

READING GUIDE FOR NEWBERY AWARD BOOKS

Year of Award	Title	Author
1945	*Rabbit Hill*	Lawson
1954	*And Now Miguel*	Krumgold
1959	*The Witch of Blackbird Pond*	Speare
1963	*A Wrinkle in Time*	L'Engle
1970	*Sounder*	Armstrong
1978	*A Bridge to Terabithia*	Paterson
1983	*Dicey's Song*	Voigt
1984	*Dear Mr. Henshaw*	Cleary

Can you find out the current Newbery books for the last few years?

1985

1986

1987

TARGET ACTIVITY

Frederic G. Melcher added the Caldecott award in 1938 for the most outstanding illustrations in a children's book. It was named for Randolph Caldecott (1846-1886), an English illustrator, painter, and sculptor, who gained a reputation for his illustrations in children's books.

Examine the Newbery or Caldecott medals that appear on the front cover of each award-winning book. Create a new medal that would combine excellence in writing *and* illustrating. Name the medal after yourself!

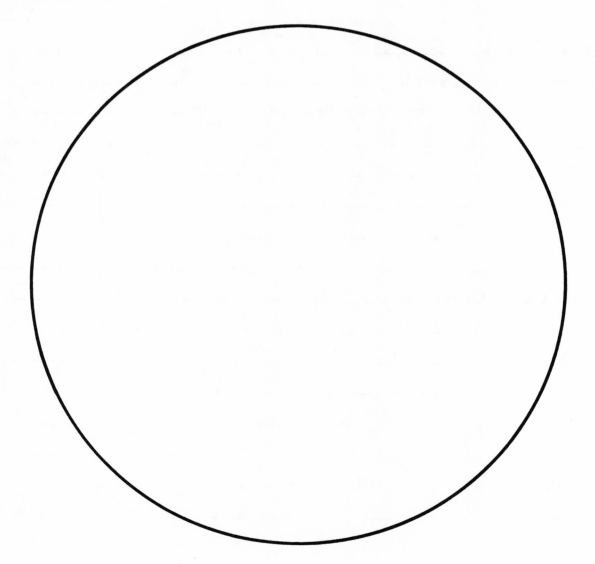

TARGET ACTIVITY

Finish reading the Newbery book selected in Target Activity 1. Fill out the analysis sheet and write a one-paragraph review when the analysis has been completed.

ANALYSIS SHEET

1. The book I have chosen is _____ .

2. The main characters are _____

   _____

3. The setting of the story is _____ .

4. The main theme of the story is _____ .

5. If I could change the story or create a new ending for it I would _____

   _____

   _____

   _____

   _____

   _____

6. The best part of this book was _____

   _____

   _____

   _____

   _____

   _____

7. On a scale of 1 to 10, I would rate this book a _____ .

8. The author is _____, and received the award for this book in 19____ .

TARGET ACTIVITY

YOU are the book! Prepare a tape telling what is in your pages and why you should be read! Use the award book you are reading, or select another to read for this activity.

SPINOFF SELECTIONS

Select one of these topics for further research about Newbery and Caldecott award winners.

history of children's literature
early children's games
Colonial primers
series books:
    Nancy Drew
    Bobbsey Twins
    The Hardy Boys
Mother Goose

chapbooks
hornbooks
picture books
John Locke
Beatrix Potter
Jacques Rousseau
Kate Greenaway

Use this space to record your information.

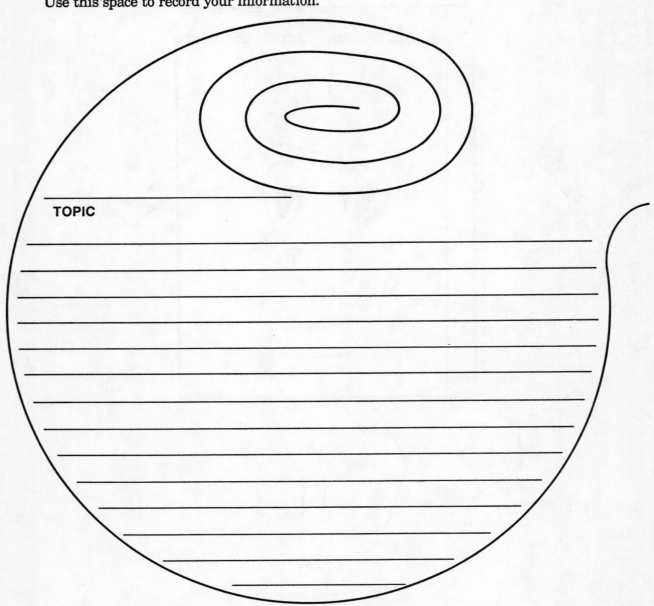

TOPIC

TAKE ACTION

Make a "Suggested Reading List" for other students your age. Use a variety of books from this section for the list. Divide the list according to book category. This will be a helpful list for others who need to do book reviews or reports for their teachers.

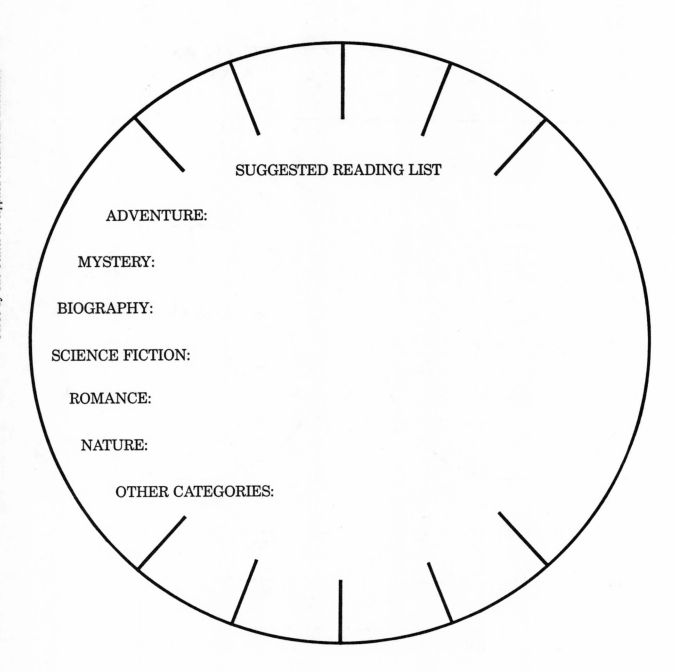

SUGGESTED READING LIST

ADVENTURE:

MYSTERY:

BIOGRAPHY:

SCIENCE FICTION:

ROMANCE:

NATURE:

OTHER CATEGORIES:

CONTRACT

Poetry. What is it? Who knows? Eleanor Farjeon, a poet, tried to answer these questions in a poem of her own. Many people consider poetry a word bargain since a powerful message can be created with a very few well-chosen words. Other people consider poetry a first cousin of music since it shares the characteristics of rhythm, line, meter, and mood.

My Target activities will be:

_____

_____

_____

My Spinoffs will be:

_____

_____

_____

I will Take Action by:

_____

_____

_____

My study will begin on _____.

Date

My goal is to finish by _____.

Date

_____   _____

Student Signature   Teacher Signature

TARGET ACTIVITY

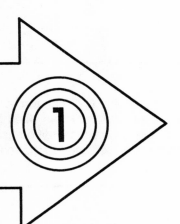

Each generation of children finds a poet with a special appeal to them. Shel Silverstein is a poet for the 1980s generation. Compare a volume of his work with a favorite of another generation, such as Robert Louis Stevenson's *A Child's Garden of Verses.*

By: Shel Silverstein   By:_____

LIKENESSES   DIFFERENCES

After reading both poetry books, I think _____

_____

_____

_____

_____

TARGET ACTIVITY

Do you like contrasts? Then the diamante poetic style is one you will enjoy. When you follow the rules below, you will have a diamond-shaped poem in which the difference between your starting noun and ending noun is explained to the reader.

Create a Diamante

Line 1 – choose a noun.

Line 2 – choose two adjectives to describe this noun.

Line 3 – choose three participles, or verbs ending in -ing, describing the Line 1 noun.

Line 4 – Use four nouns. The first two relate to the noun in Line 1 and the last two relate to the noun used in Line 7.

Line 5 – choose three participles, or verbs ending in -ing, describing the Line 7 noun.

Line 6 – choose two adjectives to describe the Line 7 noun.

Line 7 – choose a noun that is the opposite of the Line 1 noun.

Books
Fiction, Nonfiction
Writing, Publishing, Reading
Authors, Libraries, Theaters, Actors
Rehearsing, Filming, Viewing
Animated, Real-Life
Movies

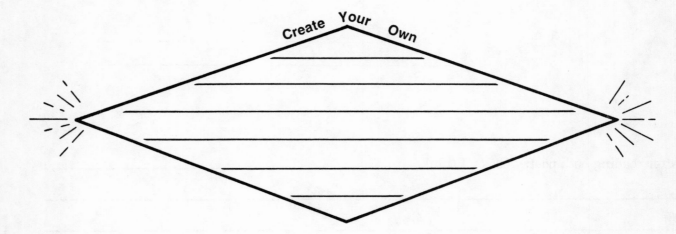

Create Your Own

Write several diamantes on colored paper cut in diamond shapes. Decorate a box to resemble a jewelry box and use this to store your poetic "jewels" for sharing.

TARGET ACTIVITY

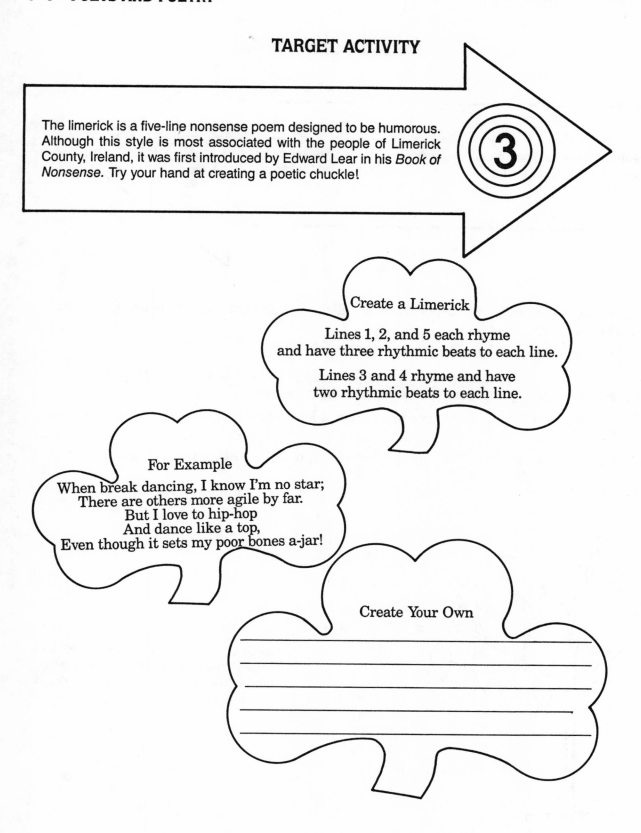

③

The limerick is a five-line nonsense poem designed to be humorous. Although this style is most associated with the people of Limerick County, Ireland, it was first introduced by Edward Lear in his *Book of Nonsense.* Try your hand at creating a poetic chuckle!

Create a Limerick

Lines 1, 2, and 5 each rhyme
and have three rhythmic beats to each line.

Lines 3 and 4 rhyme and have
two rhythmic beats to each line.

For Example

When break dancing, I know I'm no star;
There are others more agile by far.
But I love to hip-hop
And dance like a top,
Even though it sets my poor bones a-jar!

Create Your Own

_____
_____
_____
_____
_____

Write limericks of your own and/or collect limericks from poetry books. Hold a "Limerick Laugh-Off" by reading these poems aloud and judging which one gets the most chuckles.

TARGET ACTIVITY

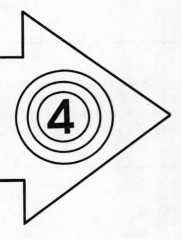

Create a "Poet-Tree" as a display for poets and their works, or for original poetry written in certain styles. Use the checklist to prepare the display.

Select a sturdy tree branch and anchor it in a container, or construct a tree from art paper and attach it to a wall.

Design and cut out leaves to attach to the branches.

Write interesting facts about the poet's life and writing style on the leaves. Include examples of famous poems written by this person or written in the person's style.

Attach the leaves to the "Poet-Tree" and provide extra leaves to encourage your classmates to add a poetic leaf.

Change the theme of the "Poet-Tree" every month to represent a new poet, a new style of poetry, or a new type of collection.

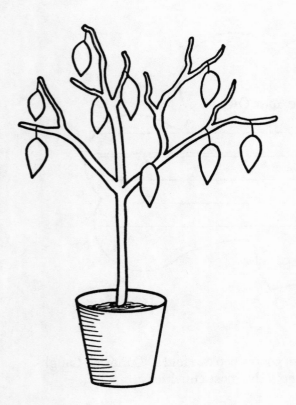

As "new leaves" are created, and "old leaves" fall, gather them in baskets labeled for the theme and keep these as a class file.

SPINOFF SELECTIONS

Select one of these topics for further research about poetry and poets.

Shel Silverstein
John Ciardi
Ogden Nash
E. E. Cummings
Rachel Field
Emily Dickinson
Robert Louis Stevenson

Henry W. Longfellow
William Shakespeare
Theodore Geisel (Dr. Seuss)
lyric poetry
narrative poetry
nursery rhymes

cinquain
haiku
David McCord
Bliss Carman
Langston Hughes
John McCrae

Use this space to record your information.

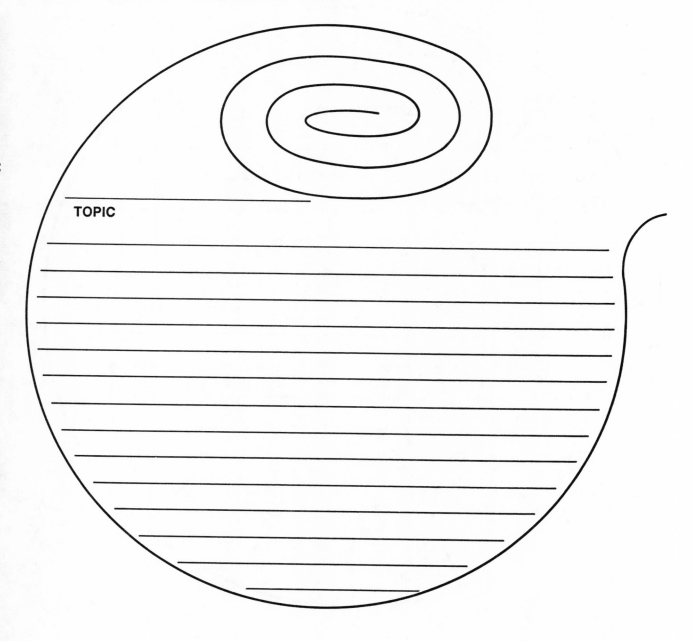

TOPIC

TAKE ACTION

To stimulate an interest in poetry, organize a poetry contest for your class, grade level, or school. Encourage students to select an interesting poem to recite and to dress in character for the recitation.

Plan the contest in the space below. Be sure to get permission for the contest, before inviting others to participate.

CONTEST TITLE

_____

DATE / TIME: _____ LOCATION: _____

LEVELS OF COMPETITION: _____

_____

RULES FOR JUDGING: _____

_____

JUDGES: _____

_____

AWARDS: _____

_____

PERMISSION GRANTED BY: _____